DOSING AMANITA MUSCARIA
And What to Expect

by Amanita Dreamer

Published by Amanita Dreamer Publishing, Ball Ground, GA

Copyright © 2023 by Amanita Dreamer
All Rights Reserved

Do not duplicate in whole or in part without prior authorization from the author

Printed in the United States of America

ISBN #: 979-8-9882966-2-1

Cover Designed by Ryan Bayron & Amanita Dreamer

to Freya,
my feline familiar

Contents

a. Important Note for You   1

b. Introduction   3

PART 1
Drink Me

1. **My Story**   15
   Where I Started · How I Got Here

2. **Addressing Fears**   23
   The Stigma · Toxicity

3. **What Is This Mushroom?**   29
   How to Use This Book

4. **Using the Mushroom**   33
   Preparation · Dosing · Initial Experiences

5. **Daily Diary**   43

6. **What Will I Feel?**   61
   In the Coming Days · What If I Feel…?

7. **Early Effects**   67
   Safety · Anxiety · Time Travel
   Food · Boundaries

8. **The Sentience of Fungi**   75
   The Woo Side

Contents

PART 2
Down the Rabbit Hole

9. **Fear & Exhaustion** — 85
   Anxiety · Fatigue · Self Love

10. **Sleep** — 95
    Sleep · Work

11. **Time, Part 1** — 99
    Government Time · Rushing

12. **Ritual & Rigidity** — 107
    Rigid Thinking · The Importance of Ritual

13. **Sun, Water, Earth, & Fire** — 117
    Relationship With the Earth

14. **Love & Fear** — 125
    Living Through the Heart

15. **Black & White Thinking** — 129
    Rigid Thinking · Emotional Complexity

16. **Elders & Ancestors** — 139
    Where We Come From · Banking Wisdom

17. **Networking** — 145
    Giving · Reciprocity · Networking

18. **Time, Part 2** — 153
    Blips · Time Manipulation

19. **Power & Ego** — 165
    Divinity · Owning Your Bigness

20. **Anger** — 175
    Anger is Good · Advocacy

21. **Boundaries** — 181
    Knowing Your Value

22. **High Dosing** — 189
    Advanced Dosing · Muscimol

23. **Smoking Amanita** — 203
    A Meditation

Contents

PART 3
Tea Party!

i. **Love Letters**   209
Personal Experiences from Amanita Users

ii. **References**   223

iii. **Appendices**   225

iv. **Meet The Team**   241
Who Did What & How This Book Happened

An Important Note for You

This book is for information, harm reduction, fantasy, storytelling and education only. I am not a practitioner for physical or mental health and I cannot give advice, medically or psychologically. By using this book you agree to seek professional advice from your health care professional before starting any method of care. Starting or stopping methodologies, medicines and lifestyles should be discussed with your healthcare providers. This book is not medical advice, is not a diagnosis, or a treatment plan.

I have published this book independently and do not affiliate with any sector, product, brand or ideology. I do not make any warranties or representations herein and this is published as is, where is, for what it is with current limited study and understandings of this medicine. I do not warrant that this information is current, accurate, complete or final. There are no human use studies, data, or information on this mushroom, and as such, there are no safe levels of use as defined by governing authorities.

> Nothing I say here has been evaluated by the FDA of the United States or by Health Canada or any other governing authority. The contents of this book are not intended to treat, diagnose, cure or prevent any disease. Consult your healthcare provider about anything in this book that you wish to use.

I do not bring this information as a professional with professional opinions or advice as I am not qualified to do so. Read with the understanding that I am reporting on my experiences and the experiences of others which is anecdotal information, not clinical trials, research or accepted current scientific methodology. I report on current research and data which is cited and you will read and form your own conclusions.

By using this book you agree that I, contributors, editors and others involved in this book are not liable for damages arising out of or in connection with the use of this book. This is a comprehensive limitation of liability that applies to any damages including direct, indirect, comprehensive, compensatory, consequential, loss of data, income, profit; loss of property or damage or claims of other parties. You agree to use this book at your own discretion and with your own discernment in conjunction with your healthcare provider. Do not start, stop, or limit use of any medications without consulting with your healthcare provider.

Please note: Amanita muscaira affects choline, glutamate, and GABA. If you are taking any medications that affect these pathways, please to not use this mushroom without checking with your doctor first. If you are on sleep medications like Ambien, do not take this mushroom. This is not an exhaustive list. Please do your research before using this drug.

Do not contact the author or anyone affiliated with this book for health care advice. This is practicing medicine without a license, and is illegal in the United States.

Amanita Dreamer
June, 2023

Introduction

Bad Ideas and My Beginning

When I first started my YouTube channel, the prevailing belief everywhere was that muscimol was the only drug here, that high doses were the way to use it, and that it was mostly crap. There was nothing about microdosing, nothing about a tea mix of both medicines, and a few comments about lemon tek or acid. In very small pockets of the internet were isolated cultural uses which discussed tiny pieces of dried mushroom taken in the mornings. That use was mostly unknown or ignored for grandiose bravado videos of a few people eating a mushroom raw.

> The prevailing idea that this mushroom was deadly or highly toxic was shared around the internet with words like "Look at their crazy bravery!"

All of this was deeply upsetting to me since this mushroom showed itself to be so much more than these simple and wrong concepts that permeated the entirety of the internet, including the few muscaria groups online and the leading trip forums. In a few isolated areas, people were beginning to experiment with different ways to convert using books whose content has been debunked with research and data.

I have a strong science background with bachelor's degrees in education, the sciences, and minors in various business, finance, education, and science-related fields. I went back to school to take more science classes. Overall I probably have enough classes to claim more bachelor's degrees, but I don't really care to do the paperwork. I have experience teaching and writing curricula and a small stint in a research lab. I excelled in biology, chemistry, and physics. I did citation research for professors and wrote hundreds of my own lab reports and summaries, teaching these same skills to high schoolers for eight years. I have authored my own books for educators. I say these things to say that this made reading the studies very easy for me, and to my surprise, many of them were deeply flawed in such glaring ways that I still can't understand how they were printed and published in prestigious publications and referenced so widely.

Even worse, as new research replaced old research, it seemed that almost everyone continued to discuss the old, outdated information. Even scientists continued to uphold old science and would argue with me based on that, ignoring the new data. Even more, I remain dumbfounded at mycologists who continue to spread misinformation and use bad rules of scientific reporting when speaking about this mushroom. I find this egregious and hard to take. Yet, these same mycologists are invited, still, to speak at festivals and conventions while I am seen with distrust, or wariness, especially since I began making videos on YouTube and because I was going up against prevailing traditions and the way it was always done. Speaking about the safety and medicinal value of ibotenic acid made me sketchy at best and someone very few people wanted to associate with. A few leaders in their fields who know the science embrace this work, and I am eternally grateful to them for their support.

This old, bumping into emerging new ideas and walking into those worlds with my, as yet, unfounded ideas, as new on the scene was a harsh reality, especially being newly healing and stepping into my own sense of place here. I made a lot of enemies who still, to this day, stalk me around the internet, reporting everything I do and creating accounts to harass me. I function under harsh censorship that other channels do not. I'm not being arrogant; these are just the circumstances as I slowly walk through each month and each stage of growth into this space, using muscaria, experimenting, pushing my doses and preparations along with working with emerging research, reaching out to those writing the papers and working to learn. I worked hard to help others understand how problematic their interpretations of the data were. Each time, I was confronted and mocked. I worked to begin correcting all of this misinformation that was in every nook and cranny of the internet. I regularly stopped to question myself and run my ideas past those whose grasp of the scientific method I valued and respected. I would spend months on an idea before going public with it.

Even so, I suffer deeply from imposter syndrome. It doesn't help that I must have been successful because now, my work is repeated by many in books, videos, talks online, and in comment sections. Now I am accused of stealing content from people who stole it from *me*. I guess this is a compliment. In instances where I used the research or work from another, I chose to interview them and make sure others knew where this information came from. This is how science works. To be sure, I walk on the shoulders of the giants who are the researchers and, most importantly, the elders and ancestors and the mushroom itself.

Tradition Mixed With New Ideas

Just because this is how we speak of things and the way things have been spoken of for decades, doesn't mean they are correct. The ideas of ego, time, what a psychedelic is, and even the terminology used in such a newly emerging field can be short-sighted. When you couple those things with seriously wrong reporting on the use of this mushroom, and how new the field of psychedelics are for the modern medical and social paradigm, we wind up with the ideas, and its place in healing needing attention and change.

When my work began, muscarias were spoken of in the same way psilocybin was because both are mushrooms, but there is very little both have in common. With muscarias, it was also discussed in grams. But this denotes you are using it dry. And there are very few circumstances where this would be the case. Almost all use it as a tea or full conversion, which is in liquid form. And dosing would be in small portions of this liquid, which is why I did my best to change this way of discussing muscaria use, to volume, not weight, by discussing dosing of tea and lactobacillus conversions. When you couple this with the fact that the number of actives in any one mushroom varies widely, and using one can result in a hot dose (very high number of actives), blending pieces of different mushrooms into your brew helps create a more average strength solution that makes it easier for all of us to talk about it. This is why you will see me discuss volume in this book, not grams in dosing.

When people speak of the Amanita muscaria, they call it a dissociative, or just a trash mushroom, toxic and useless. There are many reasons for this, some of which are decisions by industrial revolution era leaders to malign mushrooms in general and begin the tradition of having identification books include edibility, something other taxonomic books do not do, and the authors are rarely capable of making these decisions about such things. Other issues are trip cowboys who seek only the external adventure and visual experiences of entheogens and deem the experiences here not worth it. Still, another issue is dosing. Where most entheogenic compounds are simpler in their pharmacology and where dosing tends to be more easily streamlined, this mushroom is much more complex and variable, including time of day, time of year, and the complex chemistry of the person using it at the time.

Because it affects glutamate, choline, and GABA, it affects the entirety of the fight or flight system. This system affects breathing, vascularity, and blood flow to the brain and systemically, digestion, thoughts, and ability to think and process, adrenaline, cortisol and the stress hormones, sight, immunity and mental health, memory, and sleep. This means that finding proper doses for any individual is not a one-size-fits-most situation. What's more, as one uses muscaria, and as the healing of these complex systems begins, the dosing will change.

Even short term, building in rest days is necessary as you adapt and the medicine builds in your system. It is the opposite of pharmaceuticals, where you adapt and need more. Indeed, most people usually find that their bodies will outright refuse it at some point, feeling repulsed by the thought of trying to ingest it. Further complicating the issue is that most people are not aware that the word "amanita" is a genus name with hundreds of different species in it. This means many confuse the deadly amanitas with the Amanita muscaria simply because of the word amanita. This is probably the most difficult thing I come up against, trying to help educate that this is not the "destroy your liver" mushroom.

> *Dosing is unique to the individual.*

This is the number one thing I hear and deal with:
The conflation of the words *toxic* and *poisonous* further confuses what should be simple education. All drugs have rules of dosing and effects. Alcohol has those same rules; we know them and follow them as a society. This mushroom is no different, except that it is more forgiving than alcohol.

The next most common issue is high dosing:
Most other substances under high doses can cause you to sometimes feel very upsetting things while tripping, but usually, most folks have a good experience and come down and integrate well. Most people who deem their trips on this mushroom as traumatizing, which is a lot of people, mistakenly think that full-decarb muscimol is the one medicine here. They also mistakenly think you just dive in with high doses like you can with other entheogens. In reality, both ibotenic acid and muscimol are important medicines, serving different purposes. The best is a balance of the two with

a partial conversion. What this mushroom does in high doses, especially on the full muscimol side, can be upsetting if you haven't done much therapy or inner work on core trauma. The gift of this mushroom is that it will help you do just that. But full muscimol is the graduation of this mushroom, the more experienced place to be.

> Starting small and working your way up allows the mushroom to do the work on that inner trauma, slowly bringing you into growth and awareness so that when you finally do use the higher doses of muscimol, you are fully prepared for the lessons and healing there.

For the cannabis users:

There has been confusion about why some folks get nothing from the muscarias, and others get a lot. It took me a few years to begin to see a potential commonality, and that is cannabis use. Some cannabis users can still see some effects, but many do not. This makes me think there is a gating issue in the glutamate pathways in the endocannabinoid system. These are just ideas of mine, but I speak about them to help further ideas for research. I could be way off-base, but we need these conversations.

Hypotheses about what's causing errant testing of products and conversions, the role and importance of fats, the use of pre-compounds that will push other molecule formations in the body and create new pathways downstream, how the packaged mushroom in its whole form is necessary for the entourage effect seen in many other entheogenic substances, and the potential that the bacteria muscaria needs to grow in nature might be the same that is ingested which winds up being highly protective or necessary for the gut and crossing the blood-brain barrier, that these same bacteria create the safety of ibotenic acid through oral ingestion and are necessary for it, and that onboard bacteria might also cause some fermentation the same way ginger and other fermenters do are all just ideas I work on disseminating to create more ideas and conversations.

I speak publicly about some of these, asking for others to look at it too. I also believe in the possibility that some living medicines, once in the body, use molecules of the body to create yet still undiscovered compounds and pathways which use many compounds of the mushroom with many molecules in the body and, in this way, create third medicines that only exist while in the body and that perhaps they might be the key to the spiritual, ethereal nature of mushrooms.

What we feel under the influence isn't always what's happening.

This mushroom is deemed a dissociative. But this obsession with how something feels as the definition of what it is, is errant, in my opinion. How muscaria feels, how they work, and where they work are different.

Muscaria actually brings you deeply *into* your body. This is the medicine of the self, the ego, and reentering the body, especially from lifelong dissociative states. Many people who dissociate don't know they're doing it, or have a hard time identifying what that feeling is. Some people who like to get buzzed or trip are escaping the feelings of core issues when they threaten to surface. Most entheogens help one leave reality for a visual and emotional experience of euphoria and connectedness to things outside of us. But if they are not integrating the work and the therapy and asking the questions in shadow work, then it's just more dissociation. And this is different from using entheogens to actually just have joy. To be clear, the idea that these medicines are holy and, therefore, should only be used as medicine is yet another problematic take that stems from religious puritanicalism. Respecting a medicine does not equate to not enjoying it simply for the sake of joy and release.

The idea that visuals are psychedelics and dissociatives make you feel floaty is problematic. The definition of "psychedelic" does include hallucinations, but what is a hallucination? If it is only visual or auditory, then I posit that that's a very egocentric and also simplistic way to view a hallucination. Blind people have tactile and auditory hallucinations. Our nervous system perceives many things sensorily. After using muscaria for five years consistently, I am aware that our sense of time is also a highly important sense. I believe our ancestors valued it. And as such, we hallucinate time and remember the reality of our perceptions of time, among many other perceptions, through hallucinations of past selves, younger selves, and our place in times. As such, muscarias are very much psychedelic.

The other definition of "psychedelic" is the expansion of consciousness. Muscarias expand consciousness as much as the other entheogens, and anyone experienced in its use will give a resounding "yes" to this. The idea that the expansion of consciousness is outward is, yet again, simplistic and short-sighted. The expansion of consciousness is just as much inward, downward, through the self, and backward into the past as it is outward and into the now. And indeed, traveling deeply into the self until you fall out of the self back in time, you begin to realize how time is actually created by consciousness through existence and duality by incarnating and anchoring it in the space/time continuum. By viewing it through our humanness, we create it. The vast expansion of consciousness that happens when you pair the use of psilocybin and DMT with muscaria individually over time is an expansion that surpasses any of them on their own.

Amanita brings you into the self. The trip is less out there and more in here which is why trip tourists are not as impressed with it. The higher states and doses here not only bring feelings of floating but also glimpses into time, realities, and states of existence as it relates to the self.

If healing is the goal, then this mushroom is one of the greatest tools humans could have.

For example, you may see yourself in multiple timelines simultaneously and running scenarios in outward states of altered reality fueled by the ibotenic acid. But after these visual and outer perceptive states, the trip turns more deeply inward as muscimol takes over into states that most people won't remember. When some memories return, the overarching themes tend to be about choices made, how we reacted, how we moved, regrets, lessons, and our inner self and paths across timelines as separate from consciousness, point of consciousness, and experiencing.

Healing from these experiences is often reported as feeling safer in one's own skin, returning home, landing, understanding our past and our choices, forgiving the self, loving the self, and all of this requires going deeply inward, not outward. The most important reports to me are those of love. The overwhelming amount of love given from the mushrooms when entering these realms is something that goes beyond human words, to express or explain. Feeling the different forms of love from the different entheogens is yet another experience.

People whose inner selves have shut down, their voices silenced, and their power taken away at a young age, tend to have deeply rooted issues about helplessness, victimhood and dissociating from the self, and maybe self-loathing and shame. This mushroom can go to the root of these issues and facilitate healing at the core. It's funny that the trip bros who value ego death are likely the same ones who actually need this inner-depth experience. I am challenged on, confronted about, and looked askew at by people who think the opposite of ego death is arrogance and narcissism. On the contrary, the opposite of ego death is ownership of self, the embracing of duality, of the human experience, and living in our meat sacks with love, beauty, and power.

Ego death doesn't give anyone these traits.

An asshole and asshole behavior are just that. Anyone can take Amanita and use it to fuel their narcissism, and some do. It's the caution of this community and mushroom. It is common for people who have done very little reentering the body and learning emotional states and where those reside to become angry under the influence of muscaria or afterward. I see this more in those who use Ayahuasca regularly.

Most of us are aware of the ego-death narcissist who trips high on the obliteration of the ego and proclaims themselves the prophet of reality. This mushroom, more than other entheogens, does what seems like a contradictory thing: it brings one back into divinity and ownership of the self with power and motivation, thinking highly of the self with beauty while also creating more humility and a sense of community, lack of scarcity, and a wish for networking and embracing the collective. This is my current challenge of integration with this and my imposter syndrome. I stand in the duality of the assuredness of the things I write here and say publicly, coming from a place that feels healthy, and yet I also shame myself for it at the hint of anything confrontational. It's a work in progress.

The best-case scenario is that these medicines have roles as tools but also as teachers for us. I see it as muscarias for the deeply inner self, psilocybin for our relationships to all the living things and sentience on earth, and in high enough doses, the sentience of the galaxy and intergalactic concerns, and DMT experiences for the highest questions of existence and balance. I feel them as muscaria going deeply inward through the heart and out the back into experiencing the universe through the lens of time and the psilocybins going out the top in expansion outward, experiencing the universe through the lens of only now outside of space/time returning through the heart. I believe these medicines do the same with our realities, from deep inner healing to universal consciousness. But they are only tools. You are the other half of this partnership. This is the place where we can spring forward, out into the world, and realize our potential to be what we came here to be. With the motivation and need to expand and claim our space here. Many people who have suffered from depression, from a withering of the self, often find deep and profound healing here. And it is different from the healing of the psilocybins. It is time the muscarias found their place among the healing medicines again.

> *Embracing this ego work is important; healing from the inside and learning to sit and ground yourself back home is the key to ending panic and anxiety.*

These have been bold statements, I am aware. And you are free to see them as ridiculous. I love the "nature of reality" discussions and the role of entheogens in these conversations. These are exciting times in the remembering of our marriage and then divorce of some of the humans from living medicines. Our new renaissance back into the knowledge of our ancestors is something I feel very grateful to be a part of. This mushroom is so very ancestor-centered, and it has been humbling to learn. It has made me even more aware of the indigenous people who never forgot and are still the keepers of this knowledge.

And indeed, I am not the only one whose life has been transformed by the muscarias. Thousands of people have written to me over these years about their experiences too. Feeney and Masha's works also catalog similar experiences.

I want to be human. I love being here with my family while I watch them embrace the space-time playground, ugly losses, fun gains and all. I also value the balance with the other medicines to help me place myself rightly in the mix. I value what the psilocybin folks have so lovingly shown me and taught me about sentience and how the DMT entities have opened doors into realities I didn't know could be possible.

The hope is that my work changes the way this mushroom is perceived by society and, with the mushroom's directive, helps the world to see the potential in Amanita muscaria and their power and importance for not just humans but for all living things; living things who use muscarias and those who live with the decisions of the humans. As one who uses muscarias, I hope you find your relationship to the mushroom voice, your path through healing, and that this book helps guide the way.

Thank you for reading and being with me on this journey.

I love you, beautiful people.

Amanita Dreamer

PART 1
Drink Me

CHAPTER 1

My Story

This book is about the mushroom that saved my life.

> I'm going to tell you right now, up front, that this is hard to think about, much less write about, and it might be hard for you to read about. **If you're triggered by the topic of suicidal ideation, please consider skipping this chapter**.

I've always had panic attacks. My first one happened when I was 12. It wasn't until I was older that I learned I'm autistic, and that that had been the source of the bulk of the anxiety. Nothing I tried in the following years helped.

Panic and anxiety compound on each other, as do the side effects of living in panic and anxiety. Eight years of therapy later, I had changed a lot, but the panic and anxiety didn't really stop. Therapy did enable me to make changes in my life to reduce it, but then Hurricane Katrina happened, which ushered in a home foreclosure, bankruptcy, relocating, and raising my children in poverty. I tried everything I knew to do, but still found myself balled up in the corner of my bedroom for two days around the clock, awake in sheer terror like my house was being bombed and raided or something.

Benzodiazepines

I knew I couldn't live like that anymore. I hadn't eaten in days and had children to take care of. I knew the doctor would put me on some kind of heavy medication, but I had no other option. Indeed, he put me on the highest dose of the strongest benzodiazepine he had, because I was imploding.

It was wonderful to have relief from the panic. But I realized I couldn't live like this either. Soon, I was so drugged up I couldn't drive, I couldn't think, and I could barely speak. Eventually, I adjusted and I was able to begin living a somewhat normal life. That lasted about 5 years.

I started realizing that my normal, quick-functioning, highly intelligent, rapid-fire brain wasn't working. I was forgetting the date, messing up scheduling, and even showing up on the wrong days for things. I could no longer keep my shopping lists in my head, and couldn't retain anything I was reading. Then I started losing muscle tone. I was a competitive rock climber. I enjoyed kayaking, but my body started failing me. I started needing to take naps, my strength was declining, and I wound up having to quit my physical activities, which sent me into a pretty deep depression. Every time I backed off on the dose, even remotely, the panic would come back immediately.

After five years of being on benzodiazepines, the mental issues got so bad that people were getting angry at me and frustrated with me. I started losing friends. They thought I didn't care. I was missing phone calls, and even birthdays. I would sleep through things. I had to start bowing out of social engagements, and my life started getting really small. My children started making condescending comments like, "Well, that's just my mom. She can't help it. Her brain's just like that." I went from being their caretaker to someone they needed to take care of. I've lost count of how many times I lost my car in a parking lot and had to actually call for help to find my car. My short-term memory was gone. When cooking, I'd forget which ingredients I'd already added, or turn the oven on and forget about it. When I set alarms, I'd set them to the wrong time.

I went from being a provider to a liability.

I eventually decided I'd just figure out how to live with the panic, because I couldn't do benzos anymore. Any life would be better than this one–especially once I found a study connecting long-term benzodiazepine use to early-onset dementia. I was already missing my children's lives, and it was starting to look like, even if I got off these meds, the damage may have already been done. I started to see my future as one where I would need an indefinite, full-time, in-home caretaker while my children raised themselves and went on to live their own lives.

From Bad to Worse

After asking doctors how to wean myself off the benzos without losing my mind, and looking for remedies on the internet, I got to a point where I'd tried just about everything I could. Antidepressants, SSRIs, hypnotherapy, meditation, EMDR...they all led me back to the same place: indescribable physical pain, paranoia, drowsy days and restless nights, questioning reality, chronic disorientation, and still no answers. I got so good at looking like a normal person in public while my brain went nuts and my body maintained perpetual fight or flight. My muscles spasmed so violently I could hardly walk, and I walked around with tears in my eyes from the pain. Yet I acted normal, smiled at people, and lived as though nothing was wrong.

Four more years of my life were spent coping from one minute to the next through unimaginable terror, intrusive thought loops, physical pain, and mental fog. I wanted to hang on to my children's lives while I could enjoy them, and yet I found myself barely able to remember watching them pass through one beautiful phase after another. They only do this once. I've always been the type of mom to be present and soak it up. If it wasn't for pictures, I wouldn't remember anything about their lives from those four years. To me, that is the greatest loss. My oldest daughter learned to drive without me. She moved out of the house and off to another state without me. That's one of the most painful memories I have.

That's when I decided it was time to make some massive changes to get this under control once and for all, before it stole more pieces of my life I would never get back. By that time, my son was old enough to live without me, so I sent him to live at his father's for a while. I needed to isolate. I told my closest friends and family that I wasn't going to be in touch for a very long time. This was at the beginning of the summer.

I started going outside and sitting in the heat of the Southern United States, exposing myself to extreme temperatures. I got up every morning, got my coffee, went out to that deck, and sat in silence every day, all day, in the sun, in the heat.

I did not speak.

I would come in to eat, then go right back out to sit until the end of the day. I would come in to make dinner, eat in silence, go to bed, wake up, and repeat. I didn't use my voice; I didn't communicate with people. I did the minimum to keep my business running at the most minimal level. I lost lots of sales and a lot of money. I went through phases of loss and grieving.

The less I focused on what was happening out there and started focusing on what was happening in here, I started having these huge awakenings about choices I'd made, ways I'd coped, masks I'd worn, and things I'd tolerated–all this while moving through phases of anorexia, nausea, and vomiting.

...And Worse Still

That's when the first bout of suicidal ideation started. I had gotten to a point where I decided this was the end of the road for me. It wasn't that I didn't want to be here. It's that this was no way to live, and it was starting to look like this was the only way life would ever be for me. If the joys of experiencing the beautiful things in life weren't an option, and if I had to live in panic and anxiety 24/7, then maybe it was just time to call it. I couldn't live on the medication and I couldn't get off it. I started to think that continuing to live this way and being a burden on my family was selfish.

It felt practical. The thought process was, "If I really love my children, I wouldn't do this to them. They may not understand at first, but when I leave a letter and explain to them what kind of life I would be living, I think after they've gotten over the pain and the grieving, they'll just think, 'Well yeah, it kinda does make sense.'" So I made my plans. I wrote my letter. I got a will, I saw an attorney, and when everything was ready and everything was done, I said, "Well, I'll know when the time is right."

I grew weary of waking up every morning to another day of mental anguish and physical pain only to continue to suffer like this. I would actually wake up and say out loud, "FUCK!" every morning. I had hoped that the lack of food, the exposure to the elements every day, the medication, something, would kill me. By this point, I had put myself out on the balcony all day every day from the beginning of May to the end of September. I had been out there for five months straight. I had watched all the animals in the yard. I had watched the seasons change. I was out there sweating on hot days and wrapped in a blanket on cold nights. I learned who my bird family was and watched them raise and say goodbye to fledglings.

Eventually, I decided I would go see my daughter one more time, so I made a road trip. This would be the first time I had been away from the house other than just to run to the store. This wasn't a cry for help. I was steel in my resolve to end things when the time was right. Driving away from her when I left was one of the most awful moments of my life. On the way home, I set the date.

The day before I was to leave the planet, I got up the same as always, made my coffee the same as always, got out on the balcony the same as always, and something was different. Not at all the same as always. To this day I'm still not sure I understand what happened. I had been to the depths and back again. I had taken inventory of my whole life and made peace with it. I had gained so much wisdom and understanding about my life just from taking time to sit undistracted and listen to it. That morning on the balcony, I had the thought, "There's one thing you haven't done. You only went rock climbing to use the rocks for something. You only went to the river to use the current for kayaking. Have you ever walked in the woods, just for the sake of walking in the woods? I mean, if you're going to leave the planet, you should know the planet you're leaving."

> The best I can put it is, the accumulation of five months of silence and solitude unlocked something deep inside me.

The woods just called to me.

So I went walking.

My Beloved

Almost immediately, I came upon this amazingly beautiful, bright, red-orange mushroom. It stopped me in my tracks. I picked it. I brought it home and joined a mushroom identification group, who instantly identified it as Amanita muscaria - the Alice in Wonderland mushroom, the Super Mario mushroom...and deadly toxic.

This mushroom is found in religious art all around the world, from every era of human civilization until the rise of the Catholic church as a global superpower. So, what gives? This is not how humans treat a deadly, dangerous substance.

My research showed me that it was a GABA agonist, exactly what the benzo class of drugs are. I couldn't shake the feeling that I was led to this mushroom as a solution to everything I'd been through, all the problems I'd endured. I thought maybe, in its natural state, it might do what the benzos were supposed to do, and maybe without all the miserable side effects. It was worth a try; I had nothing to lose, and I could not deny the energy of this mushroom. I figured there must be more growing, so I got in my car, went foraging for several days, and found many of them.

My First Tea

Then came time to go about the business of figuring out how to make a tea from them. I looked online, but the recipes all conflicted. The mushroom forums didn't agree, and their stories were pretty awful. On Facebook, there were just as many different ways to make it and everyone was sure they had the right answer. I took a step back and remembered that I, myself, have a science background. I know chemistry. I know about decarboxylation. And I knew this thing would decarboxylate. So, I ignored everything online and went inside my own mind and, for the first time, left my survival up to both my chemistry background and the same voice that led me to the forest and to the mushrooms in the first place.

I listened, for the first time, to my intuition.

For lack of a better way of saying this, I could feel the mushrooms guiding me, and knew all I had to do was listen. How was this voice so strong? It was such an odd thing to experience. As I stood there looking at them with a pan and water I said out loud, "How do I do this?" And the answer rose up immediately: about a cup of water, about 15 grams, about 20 minutes. It was so specific. I didn't hesitate; I just did it. I felt guided, it felt very present and also holy, profound and deep. I smelled them cooking and, as the smell rose in the air, I started feeling like I was floating, like I was growing toward a past, like a connection forming, and also forward, like something powerful was opening in my world.

This actually scared me, and I wondered if just smelling the mushrooms cooking was causing some interaction with my medication. I strained them out, filled the container back to a full cup, and grabbed a measuring spoon. I asked again, and they said, "Start small and work your way up." I was so scared. I was shaking. I was thinking, 'What if this kills me? But if it does, it's doing me a favor.' I took about a quarter of a teaspoon and waited. I was pacing and really scared. But after 20 minutes and no reaction, I took another quarter teaspoon. After another 20 minutes I couldn't tolerate this anxiety and uncertainty anymore, so I just drank a lot of it.

My experience is in a video on my website. For this book, what is most important is that, once I began to experience what I now know was the trip, the joy in it, the beautiful love I felt, I knew something was changing in me and in my life. It was easy to let go and follow Alice down the rabbit hole.

What happened to me the next day was incredibly profound.

I woke up for the first time in my life with no panic or anxiety. I had no muscle spasms and no pain. My brain felt like my brain again. I had motivation, clarity, presence, and a deep sense of myself. All of a sudden, leaving the planet was the last thing on my mind. As overused and cliché as this phrase has become, I had the thought, 'This is the first day of the rest of my life. I'm going to be here for a while, and I've got stuff to do.' It's like I had stepped into a whole new body.

I fell to the floor and sobbed out loud, deeply, for all the years of my life that I lived in so much trauma and pain when the answer all along was so simple and had been here the whole time. I cried for the child, the teenager, the young adult, the new mother, the me who watched her children suffer, the me that had almost ended her life. I cried for all the people out there who I knew were suffering with this drug and trying to get off it, who couldn't find a drug and were also suicidal. I cried for all the people who thought something was wrong with them. And I cried because I knew my new life was going to be nothing like the one I had just left behind.

As I opened my eyes and stood up, I looked around this room that suddenly seemed so foreign to me. Every single thing in it was placed there by someone I no longer recognized. It didn't suit the me that had emerged. The word "baptism" floated up. YES, that. My own body didn't feel anything like the one I had yesterday. The experiences I had just been through were hard to even comprehend and, yet, I got to meet the ones who originally spoke to me and asked me to walk in the woods, and told me how to make and take the medicine. I felt their deep loving care. "Is this even real?", I asked myself. My cheese must be sliding off my cracker. Yet, I felt more grounded and normal than I ever had, in my entire life. I knew I wasn't crazy.

I went to the dried mushrooms I still had, picked them up, and saw them in a whole new way. Again, I started crying, holding them, seeing their power and beauty radiating. I felt their holiness and divinity. I was just in awe. I got a jar to make sure they stayed dry and put them on my kitchen table where they would hold a special central place. I used it again that night, but in microdose, and again for three more days until I got brave and listened when they said, "That's enough for a bit."

I can't tell you how to do what I did and I don't want people to follow me or make mistakes with their medicines, so I will just say that I had no more muscle spasms, no more withdrawal symptoms. I quit the Klonopin so easily, it was like I'd never taken it at all. I held onto that Klonopin for another six months out of fear, but the day I finally threw it in the trash and watched the waste removal workers dump it in their big truck and drive away, is a day that is burned into my mind.

From Good to Better

I was sold on mushrooms by that point. I started looking into how to use mushrooms to get my brain back. From Lion's Mane to Cordyceps, there are so many benefits these mushrooms want to grant us, and maybe I'll write another book about all of them. I knew psilocybin would be next, too. I have taken many doses as high as 10 grams as of the writing of this book. All the fungi have been instrumental in my healing so far.

As for today, the me that is writing this book is in a better place than the me that you read about in the beginning of this story. Better health-wise, both physical and mental. Better relationally. Better spiritually. Better socially. Better financially. Better in all the ways this mushroom wants to make you better, too.

And it's all because the Mushroom Voice gently invited me to take a walk, and I had the presence of mind to listen.

Thank you for reading my story. I hope this book serves to help you not have to worry and fear like I did and that it helps you walk the path they ask you to walk.

CHAPTER 2 — *Addressing Fears*

Are you afraid to get started? Are you afraid of using the mushroom? Before we do anything else, please write below what your current fears are with taking it.

When I teach this as a course, we discuss this out loud, stating what the fears are. I hear the same fears and they are normal. So, I am going to discuss some of them here.

> It's called the death mushroom and is associated with death, bad trips, and bad experiences.

> *In reality it is the **life-affirming mushroom** that creates **amazing experiences** when used correctly.*

> People say its color is a warning.

> *In reality the color can **entice you** with wonder and joy, to celebrate and **live life**!*

> People say it is hard to use and figure out.

> *In reality you can **take a bite** or just **make a simple tea** with it.*

Full conversion is more difficult because that side of the medicine is more profound, hard-hitting, and not for beginners. The mushroom is brilliant like that.

Do you realize that plant and tree identification books don't discuss the medicinal or edible value of those plants? Adding this feature to mushroom ID books was a political move. Who determines their status in a mushroom ID book? No one but the author who may or may not be a mycologist, chef, chemist, or doctor. There is no oversight or governing board that determines these judgements.

I could write pages about the politics of just this mushroom alone, and this one mushroom has been the most maligned and wrongly discussed in history. I wonder why. Allow that to inform your fear. Maybe what you have before you in this medicine is incredible power. Maybe it is an answer, not a problem.

Mushroom Fears

I get it, though. Mushrooms are highly suspect, feared and mysterious. But this mushroom is the best gateway mushroom in the world. It is so easy to identify, so easy to use, and so transformative. Once you get to know it, it will invite you into the world of the fungi, and down that rabbit hole you can go. It's a deep one and, eventually, I became enamored of the fungi. Today I live in awe and reverence of their majesty, beauty and power.

When it comes to entheogens, we are also afraid, and rightly so. Very few people can accurately describe their experiences, so it seems people go to strange lands that we can't adequately prepare for. We hear stories of people having bad experiences or suffering long-term harm.

But I can help allay your fears by telling you, many bad experiences can be attributed to either preparing it wrongly, taking way too much of it at once, or both. Let me say, when I say too much, I mean super high doses.

Before taking the really high doses, you should start small, the way you are doing here. Become familiar with it over the course of microdosing and macrodosing, and later you can push your doses into the high range. At that point you will have developed a good understanding of the Mushroom Voice and how your body works with this. You will know intuitively when you are ready. As this mushroom works to heal your body. You will gain the knowledge and experience to work with it on higher levels. I say that for a reason. This is why you hear those stories of bad experiences. People started large and weren't prepared.

I'll say it again and again: don't start large with this one.

Of all the medicines I have worked with, this mushroom is hands-down the most loving and forgiving and capable. When I took it, it was the first entheogen, the first living medicine I had taken. I was in no condition to be traumatized by a bad experience. This mushroom held me, loved me, and gently showed me more love in one experience overnight than any human, experience or medicine ever had.

Feel free to use the following list with your doctor.

> At this point, what fears do you have about taking it?
>
> ☐ I'm afraid I will make it wrong.
> ☐ I think I'll dose it incorrectly.
> ☐ What if I'm the exception?
> ☐ What if I have a weird reaction to it?
> ☐ What if it doesn't work so I take too much to try to find my dose?
> ☐ What if it's the wrong mushroom and I get sick?
> ☐ What if I have a sensitivity to ibotenic acid?
> ☐ What if it goes bad or I cook it too long?

These are normal fears, and are all entirely valid. I have built-in protections to help you avoid taking too much. I have a chapter on finding your dose. There are vendors on the website, AmanitaDreamer.Net, who I have vetted. These vendors have been harvesting this mushroom for years in the same area. When this mushroom spoils, it will smell so bad you won't be able to use it. Or the active ingredients will just slowly become inactive, and the mushroom will lose its smell completely.

I hope that this has helped you with some of your fear. For the rest, I hope working with it will help inform you.

CHAPTER 3 — What Is This Mushroom?

When people think of psychedelic mushrooms, they often think of psilocybin. This is not found in Amanita muscaria. This mushroom has two active ingredients of interest:

- **Ibotenic acid**
  (most prominent in its natural state)
- **Muscimol**
  (ibotenic acid converts to this)

Ibotenic acid affects the cholinergic and glutamate pathways (the stimulant "upper" side). Muscimol uses the GABA pathways (the sedative "downer" side).

While these two chemicals have their own unique effects on human nervous systems and brain chemistry, they combine to synergistically create a wholly separate experience when taken together. That's what this book is about. I will cover the use of them as separate things later in the book but, for most of this work, you will use the partial conversion, which is a mix of both.

It's Stigmatized

As of the writing of this book, ibotenic acid science is outdated, problematic, and inconclusive on toxicity. As with all things, the poison is in the dose. Toxicity is easily avoided with proper preparation, and proper preparation is simple.

So why is everyone pretty much unanimous about this mushroom's toxicity? In a nutshell, it really comes down to lack of research, anecdotal stories of people overdosing when misusing the mushroom for recreational purposes, and identification books choosing to include edibility information for mushrooms when they don't do this for any other type of living thing. And this practice is full of political and other agendas.

The point of this book is to create a place where ancient and modern lore can commingle with science-based information, to hopefully bring the gifts of this mushroom to offer to as many people as possible while minimizing the risks inherent in uninformed or mal-intended misuse.

It's an Adaptogen

An adaptogen is a substance (usually an herb or mushroom) that balances systems, chemical pathways, and regulatory feedback loops in the body to help maintain homeostasis in the face of stressors.

> The medical community at large is conflicted about whether or not adaptogenic benefits are anything more than the placebo effect.

Medically speaking, adaptogens are considered "non-specific," meaning they don't target any one system of the body. Academic literature treats this as a reason to downplay or entirely dismiss their benefits when, in actuality, that's the very thing that makes them so effective.

Affecting a wide range of systems like the immune system, the endocrine system, the circulatory system, the digestive system, as well as the nervous system, adaptogens can be extremely effective at creating balance in our entire bodies instead of only treating individual systems.

The autonomic nervous system (ANS) essentially manages all the programs that "run in the background," and is divided into subsystems. One of these subsystems is called the sympathetic nervous system (SNS),which is responsible for survival in dangerous conditions. It triggers what's known as the "fight or flight" response, narrowing focus, heightening attention, and optimizing the body and brain to respond to threats. Its partner subsystem, the parasympathetic nervous system (PNS), is responsible for getting us into "rest and digest," which is the exact opposite of "fight or flight."

With your SNS pulling you into survival mode and your PNS pulling you into relaxation mode, there's a constant balance going on in your nervous system. The conversation between these systems is what we mean when we talk about homeostasis and balance. Amanita muscaria can help create this balance, which is why I classify it as an adaptogen. This statement is my experience and not substantiated by research or data.

Remember those two key actives we talked about? The ibotenic acid can create effects similar to what you'd see in stimulants. Muscimol affects GABA and we know that GABA puts you in a state of "rest and digest." This is what makes it such an incredibly versatile medicine, as it can be prepared as a stimulant, sedative, or balancing agent, depending on the ratio of actives you use.

It is my opinion only that this mushroom, like other entheogens[1], seems to heal the brain rather than harm it. If it repairs your neural pathways and brings harmony to your neurochemistry, you need less and less over time. And indeed people report a repulsion to it periodically.

How Do I Take It?

The most common methods of using Amanita muscaria as reported by me, indigenous and cultural use, and modern use are:

Drink the tea
For micro- and macro-dosing

Smoke it
For relaxation and spiritual expansion

Eat it (in small doses)
For use as a stimulant

Rub it in
For topical use for many symptoms

Take Amanita products
Tinctures, gummies, shots, chocolate, etc.

As this book will focus exclusively on micro- and macrodosing, we will be focusing on the tea method and products. I have curated a vetted list of vendors of products at AmanitaDreamer.net.

How to Use This Book

This book is part information, part workbook, and part journal. It's meant to facilitate the formation of a partnership between you and the mushroom.

The journey you're about to embark on is a slow process that can't be rushed. You may be tempted to blaze through the content in these pages and jump in with both feet as soon as possible. First, that's not how Amanita works, and, second, it's a potentially dangerous way to go about it. These are potent chemicals, and you need to have a healthy respect for their ability to alter your brain chemistry when approached correctly.

So, please, be in the present, stick with the process, and let it go at its own pace. This book should take several months and the Amanita may take a year or more to fully realize your potential. You've already invested money into this book, and you've invested emotional energy into receiving the information herein. Now, choose to invest your time, so you can create with intention the experience available to you.

I ask that over the next two months, you allow the mushroom and this book to help you make some new courageous choices that you and your health care provider can discuss. You did not wind up full of fear and anxiety by accident. It's partially how your life circumstances have treated you, and partially the choices you've made in response. Use this as an opportunity see how the Amanita can lead you into a new life where fear, trauma, and suffering are replaced with groundedness, peace, and a deep-seated understanding that the life you dream of is worth living through your heart! If you read this book all at once, go back, take your time, and work through it, spending a week on each chapter of Part 2.

---

[1] "Entheogen" is a word you'll become familiar with as you work through this book. It's a way to describe psychoactive elements, but with an emphasis on spiritual awakening rather than recreational use. If you take it at a rave, it's a psychedelic; if you take it in a shamanic ceremony, it's an entheogen – even if it's the same chemical.

CHAPTER 4

Using The Mushroom

This chapter is most likely the main reason you got this book in the first place. If you skipped straight here, please go back and read the chapters before this one.
The purpose of this chapter is to educate you about experimenting with Amanita, harm reduction and building the unique relationship you need with the mushroom.

Dosing

You may get tired of reading this, but it bears repeating: *your dose is your dose*. It's not my dose or anyone else's. As such, no one can tell you what your dose should be. We'll get into macrodosing later in the book. What we need to do now is find your microdose.

Microdose

The prefix "micro-" in the case of entheogens means "a fraction of a regular dose." Most consider a microdose to be one tenth of a trip dose. The problem here is that since Amanita muscaria is so highly variable, everyone's trip dose is different. It's not even a "one size fits most" situation; it's "one size fits one."

Microdoses are usually sub-perceptible, meaning you shouldn't feel anything on your microdose. What you're looking for is a general feeling of relaxation, a reduction in anxiety, and maybe even a slight boost in energy and motivation to get things done, feel accomplished, and slip into a well-earned slumber. If you start to feel even remotely floaty, you've entered the realm of macrodosing.

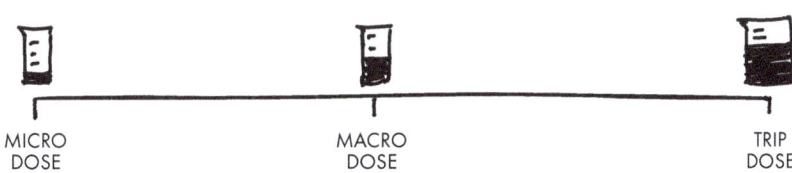

Macrodose

Your macrodose lies somewhere close to the median between your microdose and trip dose. If this were a conversation about the effects of alcohol, your micro is when you've had just enough to have loosened up a bit, your macro is when you've got a good buzz, and your trip dose is when you're belting out a '90s karaoke song with a complete stranger at 2am.

Macrodosing has an important place in the spectrum of healing this mushroom can bring. Things you should start to feel when you've found your macrodose are silliness, lightness, joy, and spontaneous laughter. When I'm using tea or any product that is a good 50/50 of both ibotenic acid and muscimol, I feel motivation to dance or work or clean or get busy. Some report a feeling of rising up or being lifted, as well as a shift in how they perceive where they are in time and space. You might get blips of time jumping momentarily or, lose time, or forget what time or day it is. Some people start sweating if they are more sensitive to these actives. Keep in mind that macrodosing is a large range from small amounts of these feelings to the larger side of macrodosing where these get more exaggerated.

You may be getting close to your trip dose if you experience any of these things to an extreme degree - losing your short-term memory and not knowing how you got where you are, forgetting what time (or even day) it is, or experiencing significant impulsivity.

Macrosoing is a very important part of this experience and will be included as part of this discussion. As you move through this book, if you feel like you are not making progress, it might be time for your macro experience. Please ask your health care professional's opinion before progressing by your 4th week.

Preparation

As mentioned before, there are several ways to take this mushroom, and each has its own unique preparation method. For the purposes of this book, we will be focusing on the tea method, which is fairly straightforward. But before I can tell you how to make the tea, there's one more important detail we need to cover: drying.

Drying the Caps

We keep the caps dry to protect the active ingredients which oxygen and moisture can quickly break down. Make sure to store your mushrooms in a jar with an airtight lid. Use a desiccant packet if you have any. If your caps arrive a little bendy, dry them until they are cracker dry. If you use an oven, put it on the lowest setting, open the door, place a fan on it and keep a keen eye on it. Check for them to be "cracker dry" before storing.

Hot Dosing

The amount of active ingredients in Amanita muscaria mushrooms varies wildly from one specimen to another. For this reason, make sure to use pieces from several different caps when making the tea. This helps balance out the mixture of ingredients and strength of the tea.

More About Dosing

Finding your dose is the hardest part. When trying to find your microdose, start small and work your way up. Using the infographic, discuss your starting dose with your health care provider.

> *Being affected by a small dose of Amanita won't make you a "lightweight," and only feeling effects from larger doses isn't something to brag about.*

Everyone's body is different, and the intent of this journey is for you to land on whatever dose works for your body, however large or small that dose may be.

Keep in mind that you are not looking to feel like you took several shots of alcohol. This is predominantly a microdosing book. A relief from fear and thoughts, a sense of relaxation, and a boost in motivation with a sense of peace is what you would be looking for. Long term effects can be created at these low doses, regardless of what your body effect feels like.

And remember, the size of your dose isn't the only thing that has a bearing on the

Making the Tea

Ingredients

- 15g of dried mushroom caps
  Use pieces from every mushroom you have. Chemical concentrations vary from cap to cap, so using pieces from each one helps give you an average amount of the active ingredients.

- 1 cup / 236 ml clean water

Instructions

1. In a small pot, simmer for 20 to 30 minutes on low.
   The larger the pot, the shallower the water - you want the caps to be completely covered. Keep an eye on it to make sure the water level doesn't drop beneath the tops of the mushrooms. Even if you put a lid on it, it's best to check periodically and top it off as needed.

2. Strain the mushroom out.

3. Add more water to bring it back up to 1 cup / 236 ml and distribute evenly between four containers with airtight lids.

4. Store three containers in the freezer for use later, and store the last one in the refrigerator.

NOTE: Lemon juice can boost the ibotenic acid conversion percentage, but it also decreases shelf life. If you want to use lemon juice, add it to the cup/dose you're currently taking, not to any of the stored containers.

strength of your tea. Play with your conversion rates. Try simmering a little longer. Try adding more lemon. Everyone's brain chemistry is unique. So, play with the recipe and raise your dose in small amounts. Again, this is the hardest part.It will also change over time as you do.

Tea Dosing Decision Guides

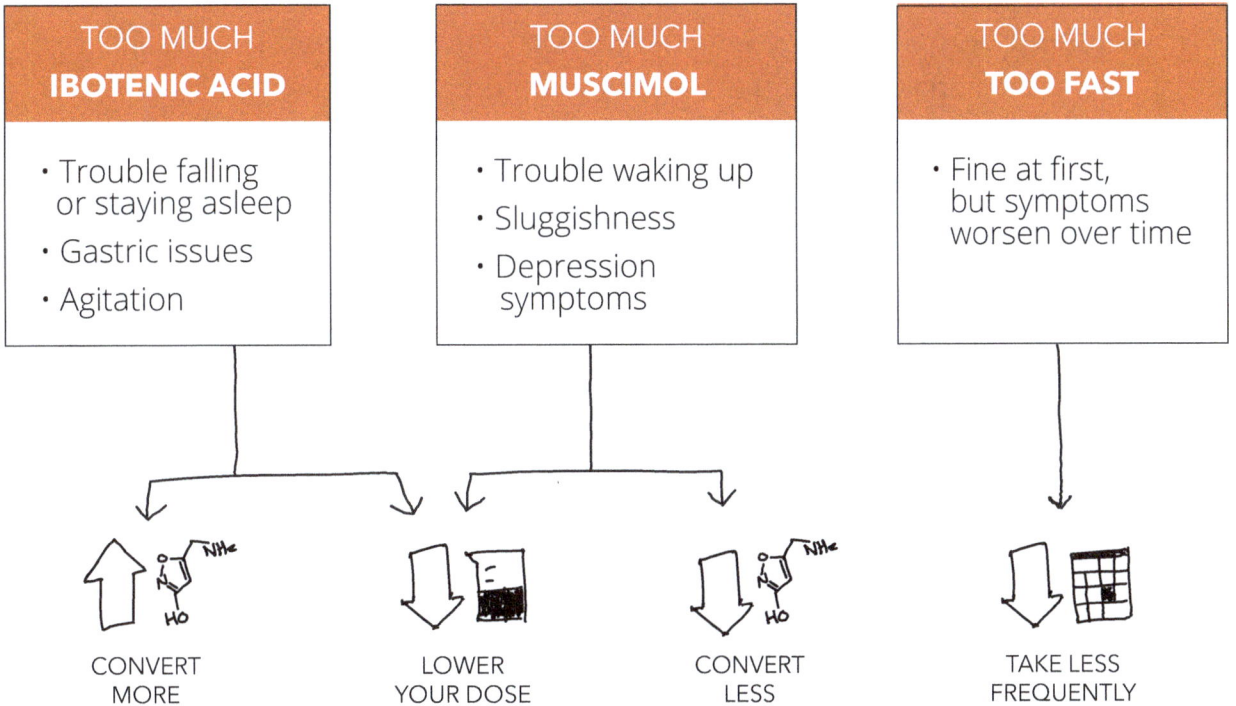

Go Slow

You'll need to find these dose sizes for yourself through trial and error. All the horror stories you hear of people having bad experiences with this mushroom are from people starting with high doses which were not correctly prepared.

Amanita deals well with incidents that occur from pre-birth to around ages six or seven, stuff your psyche locked in a vault. The contents of that vault is one of the sources of life beliefs and triggers.

Talk therapy, EMDR, and hypnotherapy work to uncover these areas, but this mushroom is like a laser going right to the root. For this reason, it is an adjunct to these therapies which you can discuss with your healthcare provider. It can be upsetting to dive in deep with a full muscimol high dose, which is why you hear scary stories from folks recovering from doing that before they were ready. So please, scoot before you crawl, crawl before you walk, walk before you run, and run before you fly. It can be magical and transformative if you've done the proper groundwork.

The Protocol

I followed this protocol for myself with information from several sources, including literature on traditional use protocols, my own experimentation, the small amount of available academic research on how ibotenic acid and muscimol are metabolized in the human body, many original cultural uses and those close to me. I then compared notes with others, collecting about 2,000 personal accounts over a four-year period. That makes me a reporter here, not your doctor, shaman, or medical advisor. Feel free to change this up as you see fit, with the spirit of using less over time at the forefront of your intentions.

- Every day for 3 days
- Every 3 days for 3 weeks
- Every 5 days for 5 weeks
- Every 10 days indefinitely
  (until you no longer need it or want to start over)

Diet and Time of Day

When you take amanita matters. It seems to have a more stimulating effect earlier in the day, and can have a more relaxing effect in the evening.

There is no limited diet with this mushroom or food to avoid. Like anything else you take, it gets into your system faster on less food and slower with food. When you're experimenting with macrodose levels, having a little food might help the ibotenic acid absorb more slowly but it won't change how sensitive you are to ibotenic acid or where your limits are, which will change over time.

Ibotenic acid cannot reform in your gut if you drink soda. I have no idea where the myth that ibotenic acid came from, but you should know there are no dietary issues.

Here's an example of what it would look like if you started on August 1:

AUGUST						
1	**2**	**3**	4	5	**6**	7
8	**9**	10	11	**12**	13	14
15	16	17	**18**	19	20	**21**
22	23	**24**	25	26	27	28
29	30	31				

SEPTEMBER						
			1	2	**3**	4
5	6	7	**8**	9	10	11
12	**13**	14	15	16	17	**18**
19	20	21	22	**23**	24	25
26	27	**28**	29	30		

Taking Breaks

You will notice the protocol in this book creates space between doses pretty quickly. And hopefully as you listen to your body you will sense that as well. There are no studies on ibotenic acid for humans or for oral use. I regularly put breaks in my use of Reishi, Lion's Mane, and Cordyceps mushrooms, as well as this one.

The only studies on this mushroom have been animal studies and are problematic. Again, there are no human, oral, ingestion, research studies. Russian protocols use the mushroom raw or dried daily for longer periods of time. The book by Baba Masha is a report on humans surveyed and is a good reference for you and your health care provider. These are all cited at the back of this book.

So just pay attention to your daily use and work to put days in between your doses. I go through periods where I do this protocol and use it in between dosing days as a macrodose and high dose when I am going through something. Outside of that, I take microdoses here and there. I high dose for ceremony on equinoxes and solstices. I use psilocybin in high doses then immediately use amanita to help with the anxiety of integration. I am healing from a lifetime of severe trauma. Even so, I put space in between not just of the medicines but of working so hard and healing work and integration therapy.

Play is important too. So is rest. Hopefully you won't need this much deep work. But if you do, remember to take breaks. I am not a doctor and this is not medical advice and not your advice. Please use testing periodically as I do, to keep tabs on your health and work with your healthcare provider.

MN NICE
ETHNOBOTANICALS

Amanita Dreamer's most trusted source for
Amanita muscaria and other ethnobotanicals in the U.S.

mn-nice-ethnobotanicals.com

CHAPTER 5

Daily Diary

The following pages are for you to use to progress through the protocol. Use them on dosing days. You can use this diary to keep a record as you go so that you can track how things change. You might want to tweak some things if you don't see changes where you want. This makes note taking convenient for taking to your health care professional.

DAY #1 — Dose Taken _____ Time _____

Mark how intensely / frequently you experienced these today.

Symptom	NOT VERY NOCTICEABLE ⊖ ——— VERY INTENSE ⊕
EXAMPLE - 60%	⊖ · · · · ♡ · · · ⊕
Anxiety	⊖ · · · · · · · · ⊕
Intrusive thoughts	⊖ · · · · · · · · ⊕
Jumpiness	⊖ · · · · · · · · ⊕
Muscle spasms	⊖ · · · · · · · · ⊕
Restless legs	⊖ · · · · · · · · ⊕
Lack of motivation	⊖ · · · · · · · · ⊕
Cravings	⊖ · · · · · · · · ⊕
Overwhelm	⊖ · · · · · · · · ⊕
Trouble sleeping	⊖ · · · · · · · · ⊕
Lack of Dreaming	⊖ · · · · · · · · ⊕
Body aches	⊖ · · · · · · · · ⊕
Hopelessness	⊖ · · · · · · · · ⊕

If you are taking your doses in the evening for stress, sleep, calming etc, the 50% decarb can give you some energy. Personally, I take mine at least 2 hours before I want to fall asleep. In that time, I use the energy I get to clean the house, do some reading and journaling. When I start to feel like I am slowing down, I lower the lights and get

---

DAY #2 *Dose Taken* _____ *Time* _____

Based on *how you feel right now*, no matter what time it is or when you took your dose, mark how intensely / frequently you experience these.

- Anxiety ⊖ · · · · · · · · · ⊕
- Intrusive thoughts ⊖ · · · · · · · · · ⊕
- Jumpiness ⊖ · · · · · · · · · ⊕
- Muscle spasms ⊖ · · · · · · · · · ⊕
- Restless legs ⊖ · · · · · · · · · ⊕
- Lack of motivation ⊖ · · · · · · · · · ⊕
- Cravings ⊖ · · · · · · · · · ⊕
- Overwhelm ⊖ · · · · · · · · · ⊕
- Trouble sleeping ⊖ · · · · · · · · · ⊕
- Lack of Dreaming ⊖ · · · · · · · · · ⊕
- Body aches ⊖ · · · · · · · · · ⊕
- Hopelessness ⊖ · · · · · · · · · ⊕

Notes (changes, worries, fears, positives, what's happening in life, questions):

horizontal. These clues seem to really help my body sort of click with the medicine. You can do these daily check-ins in the evening or as part of your morning after you've read your meditation or done some exercises or a walk, whatever your morning ritual is.

DAY #3   *Dose Taken*   *Time*

Based on *how you feel right now*, no matter what time it is or when you took your dose, mark how intensely / frequently you experience these.

- Anxiety ⊖ · · · · · · · · ⊕
- Intrusive thoughts ⊖ · · · · · · · · ⊕
- Jumpiness ⊖ · · · · · · · · ⊕
- Muscle spasms ⊖ · · · · · · · · ⊕
- Restless legs ⊖ · · · · · · · · ⊕
- Lack of motivation ⊖ · · · · · · · · ⊕
- Cravings ⊖ · · · · · · · · ⊕
- Overwhelm ⊖ · · · · · · · · ⊕
- Trouble sleeping ⊖ · · · · · · · · ⊕
- Lack of Dreaming ⊖ · · · · · · · · ⊕
- Body aches ⊖ · · · · · · · · ⊕
- Hopelessness ⊖ · · · · · · · · ⊕

Notes (changes, worries, fears, positives, what's happening in life, questions):

DAY #4 Dose Taken _____   Time _____

Based on *how you feel right now*, no matter what time it is or when you took your dose, mark how intensely / frequently you experience these.

Symptom	− · · · · · · · · · +
Anxiety	⊖ · · · · · · · · · ⊕
Intrusive thoughts	⊖ · · · · · · · · · ⊕
Jumpiness	⊖ · · · · · · · · · ⊕
Muscle spasms	⊖ · · · · · · · · · ⊕
Restless legs	⊖ · · · · · · · · · ⊕
Lack of motivation	⊖ · · · · · · · · · ⊕
Cravings	⊖ · · · · · · · · · ⊕
Overwhelm	⊖ · · · · · · · · · ⊕
Trouble sleeping	⊖ · · · · · · · · · ⊕
Lack of Dreaming	⊖ · · · · · · · · · ⊕
Body aches	⊖ · · · · · · · · · ⊕
Hopelessness	⊖ · · · · · · · · · ⊕

Notes (changes, worries, fears, positives, what's happening in life, questions):

DAY #5 — Dose Taken _____ Time _____

Based on *how you feel right now*, no matter what time it is or when you took your dose, mark how intensely / frequently you experience these.

Symptom	− · · · · · · · · +
Anxiety	⊖ · · · · · · · · ⊕
Intrusive thoughts	⊖ · · · · · · · · ⊕
Jumpiness	⊖ · · · · · · · · ⊕
Muscle spasms	⊖ · · · · · · · · ⊕
Restless legs	⊖ · · · · · · · · ⊕
Lack of motivation	⊖ · · · · · · · · ⊕
Cravings	⊖ · · · · · · · · ⊕
Overwhelm	⊖ · · · · · · · · ⊕
Trouble sleeping	⊖ · · · · · · · · ⊕
Lack of Dreaming	⊖ · · · · · · · · ⊕
Body aches	⊖ · · · · · · · · ⊕
Hopelessness	⊖ · · · · · · · · ⊕

Notes (changes, worries, fears, positives, what's happening in life, questions):

| DAY #6 | *Dose Taken* | | *Time* | |

Based on *how you feel right now*, no matter what time it is or when you took your dose, mark how intensely / frequently you experience these.

- Anxiety ⊖ · · · · · · · · · ⊕
- Intrusive thoughts ⊖ · · · · · · · · · ⊕
- Jumpiness ⊖ · · · · · · · · · ⊕
- Muscle spasms ⊖ · · · · · · · · · ⊕
- Restless legs ⊖ · · · · · · · · · ⊕
- Lack of motivation ⊖ · · · · · · · · · ⊕
- Cravings ⊖ · · · · · · · · · ⊕
- Overwhelm ⊖ · · · · · · · · · ⊕
- Trouble sleeping ⊖ · · · · · · · · · ⊕
- Lack of Dreaming ⊖ · · · · · · · · · ⊕
- Body aches ⊖ · · · · · · · · · ⊕
- Hopelessness ⊖ · · · · · · · · · ⊕

Notes (changes, worries, fears, positives, what's happening in life, questions):

| DAY #7 | *Dose Taken* | *Time* |

Based on *how you feel right now*, no matter what time it is or when you took your dose, mark how intensely / frequently you experience these.

- Anxiety ⊖ · · · · · · · · ⊕
- Intrusive thoughts ⊖ · · · · · · · · ⊕
- Jumpiness ⊖ · · · · · · · · ⊕
- Muscle spasms ⊖ · · · · · · · · ⊕
- Restless legs ⊖ · · · · · · · · ⊕
- Lack of motivation ⊖ · · · · · · · · ⊕
- Cravings ⊖ · · · · · · · · ⊕
- Overwhelm ⊖ · · · · · · · · ⊕
- Trouble sleeping ⊖ · · · · · · · · ⊕
- Lack of Dreaming ⊖ · · · · · · · · ⊕
- Body aches ⊖ · · · · · · · · ⊕
- Hopelessness ⊖ · · · · · · · · ⊕

Notes (changes, worries, fears, positives, what's happening in life, questions):

DAY #8

Dose Taken _____ *Time* _____

Based on *how you feel right now*, no matter what time it is or when you took your dose, mark how intensely / frequently you experience these.

Symptom	− · · · · · · · · · +
Anxiety	⊖ · · · · · · · · · ⊕
Intrusive thoughts	⊖ · · · · · · · · · ⊕
Jumpiness	⊖ · · · · · · · · · ⊕
Muscle spasms	⊖ · · · · · · · · · ⊕
Restless legs	⊖ · · · · · · · · · ⊕
Lack of motivation	⊖ · · · · · · · · · ⊕
Cravings	⊖ · · · · · · · · · ⊕
Overwhelm	⊖ · · · · · · · · · ⊕
Trouble sleeping	⊖ · · · · · · · · · ⊕
Lack of Dreaming	⊖ · · · · · · · · · ⊕
Body aches	⊖ · · · · · · · · · ⊕
Hopelessness	⊖ · · · · · · · · · ⊕

Notes (changes, worries, fears, positives, what's happening in life, questions):

DAY #9

Dose Taken _____   **Time** _____

Based on *how you feel right now*, no matter what time it is or when you took your dose, mark how intensely / frequently you experience these.

Symptom	− · · · · · · · · · +
Anxiety	⊖ · · · · · · · · · ⊕
Intrusive thoughts	⊖ · · · · · · · · · ⊕
Jumpiness	⊖ · · · · · · · · · ⊕
Muscle spasms	⊖ · · · · · · · · · ⊕
Restless legs	⊖ · · · · · · · · · ⊕
Lack of motivation	⊖ · · · · · · · · · ⊕
Cravings	⊖ · · · · · · · · · ⊕
Overwhelm	⊖ · · · · · · · · · ⊕
Trouble sleeping	⊖ · · · · · · · · · ⊕
Lack of Dreaming	⊖ · · · · · · · · · ⊕
Body aches	⊖ · · · · · · · · · ⊕
Hopelessness	⊖ · · · · · · · · · ⊕

Notes (changes, worries, fears, positives, what's happening in life, questions):

DAY #10

Dose Taken _____ **Time** _____

Based on *how you feel right now*, no matter what time it is or when you took your dose, mark how intensely / frequently you experience these.

	⊖										⊕
Anxiety		·	·	·	·	·	·	·	·	·	
Intrusive thoughts		·	·	·	·	·	·	·	·	·	
Jumpiness		·	·	·	·	·	·	·	·	·	
Muscle spasms		·	·	·	·	·	·	·	·	·	
Restless legs		·	·	·	·	·	·	·	·	·	
Lack of motivation		·	·	·	·	·	·	·	·	·	
Cravings		·	·	·	·	·	·	·	·	·	
Overwhelm		·	·	·	·	·	·	·	·	·	
Trouble sleeping		·	·	·	·	·	·	·	·	·	
Lack of Dreaming		·	·	·	·	·	·	·	·	·	
Body aches		·	·	·	·	·	·	·	·	·	
Hopelessness		·	·	·	·	·	·	·	·	·	

Notes (changes, worries, fears, positives, what's happening in life, questions):

Day 11

Today we will look back over your prior answers. If nothing has improved, your dose might be too low. If you are having more spasms or stomach issues, it may be too much ibotenic acid. You might want to decarb it more by adding lemon to your dosing. If you have a product you bought, you might want to find one with a little more conversion or consider making the tea yourself so you can work with it to find what conversion fits. Full muscimol will make you have very specific issues and is not what I speak to with this book. Those are:

- Fatigue
- Difficulty waking up
- Feeling thick in the head
- Hunger
- Weight gain

This is too much unless you are wanting to feel this way while you are trying to get stabilized from extreme circumstances. In that case, you might get more from this book if you get more stable and able to work with the half decarb so that you can begin to work within the bounds of this material. Using full muscimol to get stable is certainly a path some people take.

If you are not "feeling" anything, remember that microdosing won't feel very strong. We're looking for improvement in the markers on these pages over the past ten doses. There is no one size fits all, and you will need to work with different preparations or doses until you find what fits you. I have included more of these pages in case you wish to start over again after finding your dose. They are at the back of the book.

Looking back at your answers for *anxiety*, has it improved?

Anxiety on First Day ⊖ • • • • • • • • • ⊕

Anxiety Today ⊖ • • • • • • • • • ⊕

What changes have you noticed?

Looking back at your answers for *intrusive thoughts*, has it improved?

Thoughts on First Day ⊖ • • • • • • • • • ⊕

Thoughts Today ⊖ • • • • • • • • • ⊕

What changes have you noticed?

Looking back at your answers for *jumpiness*, has it improved?

Jumpiness on First Day ⊖ • • • • • • • • • ⊕

Jumpiness Today ⊖ • • • • • • • • • ⊕

What changes have you noticed?

Looking back at your answers for *muscle spasms*, has it improved?

Spasms on First Day ⊖ • • • • • • • • • ⊕

Spasms Today ⊖ • • • • • • • • • ⊕

What changes have you noticed?

Looking back at your answers for *restlessness*, has it improved?

Restlessness on First Day ⊖ · · · · · · · · ⊕

Restlessness Today ⊖ · · · · · · · · ⊕

What changes have you noticed?

Looking back at your answers for *lack of motivation*, has it improved?

Motivation on First Day ⊖ · · · · · · · · ⊕

Motivation Today ⊖ · · · · · · · · ⊕

What changes have you noticed?

Looking back at your answers for *cravings*, has it improved?

Cravings on First Day ⊖ · · · · · · · · ⊕

Cravings Today ⊖ · · · · · · · · ⊕

What changes have you noticed?

Looking back at your answers for *overwhelm*, has it improved?

Overwhelm on First Day ⊖ · · · · · · · · · ⊕
Overwhelm Today ⊖ · · · · · · · · · ⊕

What changes have you noticed?

Looking back at your answers for *trouble sleeping*, has it improved?

Sleep on First Day ⊖ · · · · · · · · · ⊕
Sleep Today ⊖ · · · · · · · · · ⊕

What changes have you noticed?

Looking back at your answers for *lack of dreams*, has it improved?

Dreams on First Day ⊖ · · · · · · · · · ⊕
Dreams Today ⊖ · · · · · · · · · ⊕

What changes have you noticed?

Looking back at your answers for *body aches*, has it improved?

Achiness on First Day ⊖ · · · · · · · · · ⊕

Achiness Today ⊖ · · · · · · · · · ⊕

What changes have you noticed?

Looking back at your answers for *hopelessness*, has it improved?

Hopelessness on First Day ⊖ · · · · · · · · · ⊕

HopelessnessToday ⊖ · · · · · · · · · ⊕

What changes have you noticed?

Keep in mind, some Amanita more than others can make you sweat. I sweated for the first 3 years even in microdoses. Today I do when I am going through something or when I have to take doses a little higher than micro. Sleeping less, shorter hours, waking up after 3 or 4 hours with a burst of energy then going back to sleep, are all reported by many people. When you write below, please leave notes about these and any other things you have noticed.

Macrodosing

In this book, I bring up macrodosing. These pages are for recording your first macrodosing experiences, for notes and learning, and charting your progress.

Starting test dose

How long before you felt something

Note what you felt as the time progressed

Which of the following did you experience?

                    Time Jumps   Thought Loops
               High Motivation   Confusion
   Bouts of Sadness / Crying   Feeling Invincible
          Multiple Timelines   Laughter
        Feeling High / Drunk   Deep Thoughts
          Dancing & Moving   Limp Arms / Legs

List other things you experienced

Next time, do you need to go higher, decarb more, or go lower? Stomach issues would need more time simmering, more lemon, and/or more decarb to remove more ibotenic acid. If it was underwhelming, continue working with your dose upward. You can try again the next night or wait a day. This will interrupt your microdose schedule. When you are finished taking macrodoses, go five days without, then pick up your schedule where you left off. Don't macrodose more than five days in a row.

Second Macrodose

Dose   How long before you felt something

Note what you felt as the time progressed

Which of the following did you experience?

Time Jumps   Thought Loops
High Motivation   Confusion
Bouts of Sadness / Crying   Feeling Invincible
Multiple Timelines   Laughter
Feeling High / Drunk   Deep Thoughts
Dancing & Moving   Limp Arms / Legs

List other things you experienced

Do you need to change your dose up or down at all? If you started to have memory loss, inability to walk or woke up not knowing how things got where they are you have passed macrodose and are entering trip doses. You would need to have someone with you at those doses. Macrodoses should be fully manageable alone.

Third Macrodose

Dose _____ How long before you felt something _____

Note what you felt as the time progressed

_____

Which of the following did you experience?

- Time Jumps
- High Motivation
- Bouts of Sadness / Crying
- Multiple Timelines
- Feeling High / Drunk
- Dancing & Moving
- Thought Loops
- Confusion
- Feeling Invincible
- Laughter
- Deep Thoughts
- Limp Arms / Legs

List other things you experienced

_____

By now you should be feeling very comfortable with this level of dosing and really feeling the mushroom voice onboard. If not, what changes do you still need to make? If you need help, visit MushroomVoice.com and ask questions in our community.

CHAPTER 6

What If I Feel...?

If you won't feel buzzed, or any kind of noticeable mind-altering effects, what will you feel? How will you know you've found your microdose?

Right After You Take It

When you first take a microdose it will take about 20 minutes or more to have an effect. Remember that the experiences this mushroom produces vary greatly from person to person. That being said, in general, as the amount of ibotenic acid converts to muscimol in your body over time, you will slowly feel more relaxed, stress-free, motivated, and also sleepy. Mostly expect to feel comfortable and less anxious.

> *You might not feel anything at all, and that's okay—that doesn't mean it's not working.*

If you feel nothing and are working on increasing your dose each time, keep in mind that there are medicines like cannabis that can block the effects. Each body is different and it is possible to get healing without feeling much from dosing. As you approach the two tablespoon mark, consider this. Some people stop cannabis for Amanita and find it helpful.

After The First Day

Most people report feeling very awake, aware, refreshed, and well-rested. Some people wake up the next day and spring into action with whatever they need to get done that day. The medicine works differently on some, but wisely on all. Some people experience sweating during the night. If you have cramps or twitching, consider ibotenic acid and either your dose is too high or you need to simmer your tea longer. Or you might need to convert it more with lemon.

After The First Week

You might start to realize that maybe feeling good might be your new normal. You may feel like you need to take more, or increase the amount you are taking.

> It is important that you develop a relationship with this medicine and learn to listen to your inner wisdom.

With anxiety and current medicine, we learn not to do this. With mushroom medicine we must relearn how to do this. This medicine is the perfect teacher and louder than most. If you experience twitching, inability to go back to sleep after only sleeping for a few hours and sleep deprivation, some people report reducing their dose or try taking it two or more hours before bed.

In the following weeks you will start to notice "blips," or the very beginnings of things we will discuss in greater detail later in this book. As you move through your dosing, you may notice any of the following things:

- Relief of feelings of hopelessness
- Relief of anxiety
- High levels of motivation to do things you haven't wanted to do in a long time
- A desire to clear out your home, desk, life, car, closets etc.
- A need to play or stretch out your arms or sit up straighter
- A need to travel, meet more people, see more things
- "Time blips," where it feels like you popped out of time, went somewhere else, and then popped back in again
- Time adjustments where 20 minutes feels like an hour, or several hours feels like 20 minutes
- You may want more order or organization in your life but fewer compulsions or less rigidity
- You revere more things, feel loving or grateful about small things
- You might want to begin new rituals or feel the need to sit more deeply with your coffee or tea or the sunset or notice people or things that you love, or you want to stop often and really soak them up

All these things are merely the beginnings of how far down the rabbit hole your experiences can take you, how beautiful life can be, and how much control you will start to feel over your future and the life you want to live. If you do or don't feel these things, please discuss it with your healthcare professional. There are no right or wrong ways to move through this process.

After The First Month

You might start to notice the details of how things were contributing to your fears, your choices, your actions and how this mushroom is showing you the opposite of those things and how you can make better choices. Those choices may also be scary. After several months of making new choices, you might notice others treating you differently, and a return of anxiety because you are stretching beyond your comfort zone. You could start to notice positive feedback like coincidences, things you wanted finally showing up, problems becoming easier to solve, and yet new problems arising asking to finally be dealt with. You could feel more personal power and confidence, and an inability to tolerate things you once tolerated.

If that sounds awesome and you're eager to arrive there, remember that this is a long game. If you stick with this protocol, you can use what you learn to help you keep going, deeper into this book and the profound changes you will read about here.

What if I Feel _____ ?

The following questions are about microdosing.

> **What if I keep waking up sweating?**

> This seems to be a common experience and can represent a dose slightly higher than microdosing. Sweating can also be your body's natural reaction near the beginning of working with Amanita muscaria. Extreme sweating that doesn't let up can just be a dose that's too high, or maybe you need more conversion.

What if I have crazy dreams?

Wild, crazy, vivid, dark, emotive dreams are commonly reported. This mushroom works a lot in the dream state.

What if I'm taking mostly muscimol and am having a hard time thinking, getting up, or being motivated to do anything?

Yeah, that's not good. Consider you might be taking too much muscimol. Consider one of the following:

- Reduce the size of your dose
- Put more time between taking it
- Do less conversion (use less lemon).
- Use more ibotenic acid in the mix

What if I am feeling angry, agitated, and irritable?

Always discuss negative feelings with your therapist. This can be ibotenic acid letting you know you are taking too much. You might also be simply working through issues that involve anger, usually boundary violations from childhood. If it feels deep and heavy, it's likely emotional. You can always test it by putting more days between your doses. Dealing with stuff feels more emotional, while too much ibotenic acid will feel more physical.

What if I am starting to experience deeply emotional issues and having problems?

This is what integration is for. Always reach out for professional help. We have integration counselors at AmanitaDreamer.net.

Listening to your body with mushroom medicines will become a very important skill for you to learn. This is a conversation between living sentient beings. This is living medicine and will always be in flux as you work with it and as you heal.

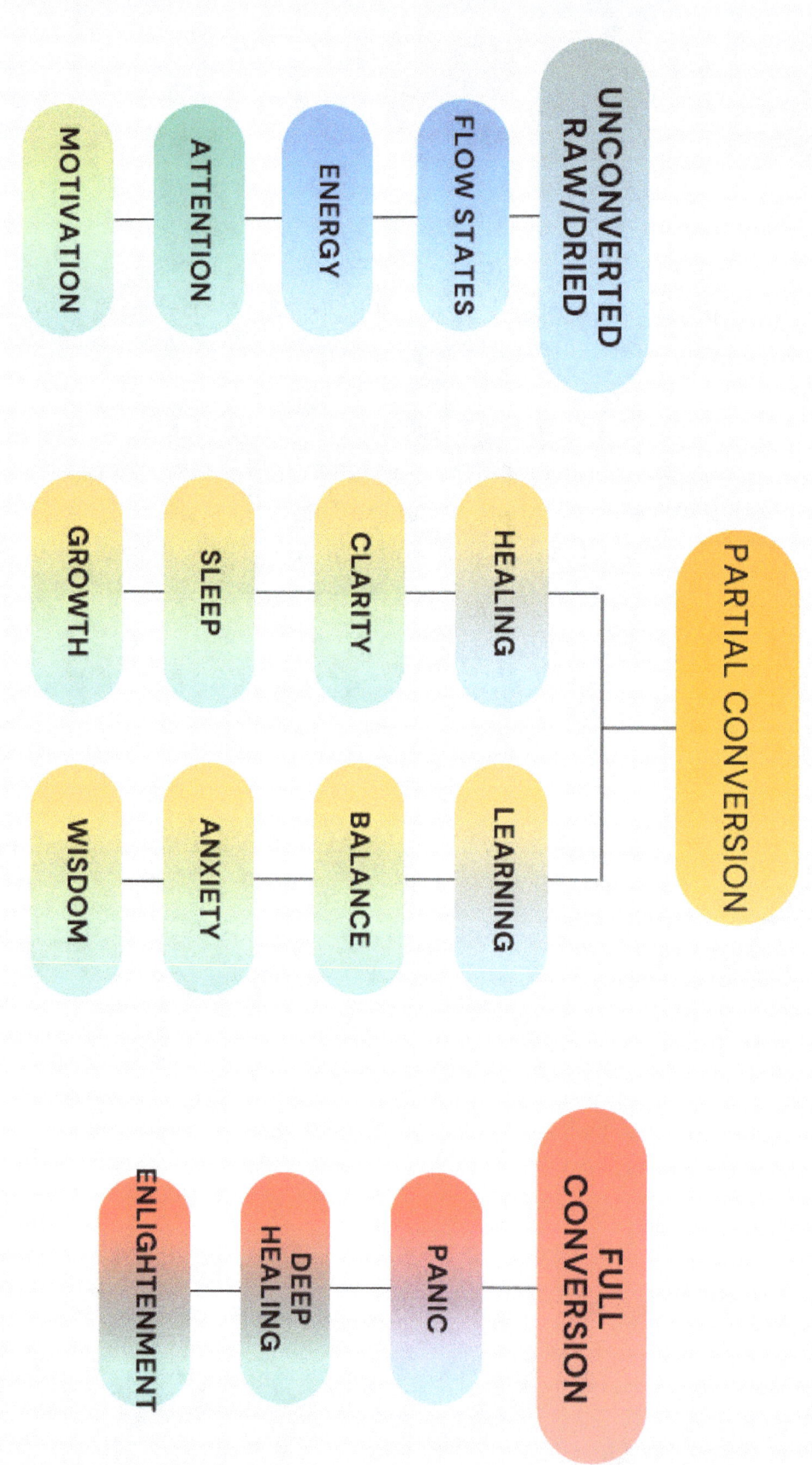

CHAPTER 7

Early Effects

I'm about to shift gears. While anxiety and depression are both very real experiences with very real consequences, they are also both your body's response to you trying to live within society. This mushroom will start there.

Think of it like money. Poverty is real. Classism is real. Trading your effort points for bank notes and knowing that the number of bank notes you've accrued will determine whether or not you can take your family on a cruise next summer is real. But if every human on the planet agreed tomorrow that money had no value, it would indeed stop having any value. Money is only as real as we decide it is. It doesn't have any intrinsic beingness outside of what we assign it.

The gear I'm about to shift to is simply that everything I just said about money is also true about time. And the Amanita helps you reframe your relationship with the concept of time. This was the very first lesson the amanita taught me and they gave me a sense of urgency about how important it was that we tackled it first.

Early Effects

Aside from the new lessons in time, most people report experiencing the following:

Safety

When you learn how to live through the heart, you'll quickly learn that the heart knows what safety is. And the only way to learn what it feels like to access that inner knowing is to become safe for yourself first.

You can only trust others to the degree that you trust yourself. If you don't trust yourself, then you don't trust your ability to deem others trustworthy. So even if you do extend trust in practice, you still can't fully trust in spirit. On the other hand, once you trust yourself to be able to tell who's trustworthy, it becomes easier to actually trust the people you choose to trust. When you learn how to protect yourself and how to speak up and how to make better choices, you will learn that safety begins inside. You and your therapist can and should discuss trust and safety in these respects.

Start by being as safe for yourself as you possibly can. And start that by refusing to rush.

Once you've adopted this lifestyle and are living from the heart, you'll find you can actually catch your breath, recover some motivation, surrender some of that hopelessness and get some quality sleep, and just actually start living like humans are supposed to live. Your body will have less need to use things like anxiety and depression to get your attention. As you start your whole health journey with Amanita, you can notice when you feel safe and when you don't, when you feel love and when you don't, when you are rushing and that it feels gross.

Sleep

Many people say they notice changes in sleep. You might sweat in your sleep. You might sleep really hard for 2 hours and wake up a lot or sleep through the night for the first time. You might have fitful dreams you don't really remember. You might have extremely vivid dreams you do remember. You might start waking up after only 4 or 5 hours of sleep feeling deeply rested and ready to start your day. All of this has been reported and, indeed, all those things happen to me too.

Fear Relief

One of the first things you might notice is relief from fear and panic. It's wonderful to feel that relief. If you're not getting that, go back to the chapter on finding your dose. This medicine can balance the complex systems involved in your fight or flight system. We have no studies on this but, with thousands of people using it and anecdotal information, indigenous use and lore, we see the balancing of these systems, making it adaptogenic. But also, over time, we need it less and less, and we need less when we take it. This conversation can lead us to make changes in our own best interest.

Time

Imagine you go for a doorknob and instead of grabbing it, you go right through it. This can be disorienting until you realize that you jumped ahead in time to where you had already opened the door and pulled it back a little, so the doorknob was closer than you thought when you grabbed for it.

These little blips can jump you one or two seconds into either the future or the past, which can be wildly disorienting at first. You'll start using handrails on the stairs and triple checking important things. Other times, you'll see a sign then when you glance away and back again it'll be gone, and then when you look again it'll be there. You either got a glimpse of the past before it was built, or saw a future where it's already been removed.

> Yes, this sounds ridiculous, and yes, this is what you'll sound like sharing your Amanita experiences with people who haven't been down this road.

The only way to really hear and accept what I'm saying is to experience it for yourself. People have told me about how they thought on Tuesday about folding their towels, and then opened their closet only to find they've already been washed, folded, and put away, and their phone says it's Wednesday. It can be upsetting and confusing at first. But now that you know about it, hopefully you can relax and think, "Oh yeah, Dreamer said this would happen." I laugh about it and think it's funny, entertaining and a beautiful reminder about how fun it is to live on Earth and how cool this mushroom can be. Of course if this is upsetting, please discuss it with your health care professional.

Coping With It

For me this lasted about a year. No worries, though, you'll get to a point where, when this happens, you can reconcile it pretty quickly. You'll know what's happening and why it's happening. This is something the mushroom does on purpose to teach you about time–what it is and what it's not–and to dislodge you from government time so you can operate according to your time. What it's going to mean, though, is you can no longer rely solely on your mind the way you're used to for the things you need to remember. Once you notice this starting to happen, you'll have to get good at reminders. If you don't know how to schedule an email, you need to learn how to do that. If you don't have a good reminder app, you need to download one. Find physical ways in your life to get things to happen. If you need to ship something tomorrow, box it up and set it by the door right now so you see it on the way out the door tomorrow.

Get good at lists, at asking for help, at purposefully taking responsibility for making certain that all time-related things are accounted for in some way. Of course if you are concerned about your memory, please see a doctor.

It could take time to fully adjust to this new dynamic. If you're going to heal, this is step number one. This is the most basic and fundamental part. Everything else we cover in this book will be built on this foundation.

Food

What Amanita has shown me personally over the years is that the trauma stored in my body made me crave sugar and the relief of pain through overdosing on nicotine in the form of government cigarettes. And I was able to get off of them almost immediately when I started using Amanita.

Sugar took a while longer. What the Amanita can do is bring you to a place where you can address your pain and fear, and asks you to match the vibration of the love that is now replacing what was once a very dark, low, toxic energy, to the point that you no longer even crave the things you were addicted to before. There's no more pain for the addiction to ease.

But Amanita has done something surprising in regard to food. I've also gotten to a point where I can tell the difference between foods that are really well-made foods and those that aren't. I can't eat boxed food anymore, or foods with a lot of additives, so I'm cooking at home most of the time now. I can't even handle corporate restaurant food because they have so many preservatives and added flavors. Amanita has helped my body remember the ancient skill of being able to smell my food and know that it's something my body will like or something that is no longer appealing or acceptable. I've always wondered how my cats smell something and walk away, but find the same food from a different source acceptable. I am growing stronger in my ability to use smell to sense the same way they do.

My family asks me to smell food and tell them if it's okay. I sometimes get nauseous just from smelling food with certain additives, preservatives, chemicals, colorings, etc. This makes me high-maintenance and makes travel more difficult. But our bodies haven't had time to adjust evolutionarily to the new things being added to our food, so some of it might not work well with our bodies. The sensitivity to have your body inform you just by smelling food is an amazing adaptation. And the ability to tap into it is a gift.

Amanita won't tell you a diet you have to keep to, it just seems to ask you to love yourself enough to just make it as clean as possible, as close to the source and the earth as possible, including the water. On the upside, knowing that the things I put in and on my body are the least harmful things possible helps my body feel soothed and taken care of and loved. And, in turn, I feel soothed and taken care of and loved. It's not always possible. Money restrictions, cultural practices of where I am at the time, my cravings, what's available, time, etc. all inform my diet. It's a do-your-best type of thing. We have limitations, and we will learn to do the best we can within those. I am only letting you know what to expect when it comes to food once you start Amanita.

Boundaries

Because Amanita is the self mushroom, honor of self, love of self, learning about self, what you'll see naturally is wanting to set more boundaries. Once you get this outside-in perspective and start marching to the beat of your own internal drum, you'll see more and more behaviors that you won't be able to tolerate because you'll not only see how they contribute to the chaos, but also the detrimental effect that chaos has on all of us.

Parallel to this, the mushroom will be helping you work through the process of dissolving all your reasons to stay quiet. Combine all these ingredients, and what you have is an advocate. You may notice yourself speaking up when you see things that hurt humanity. You may see yourself needing to say no, to set boundaries, to live by finding others' boundaries and honoring them.

I can't trust your 'yes' if
I can't trust you to say 'no.'

You may start setting boundaries for how people are allowed to treat you, and what kinds of energies you allow into your life, your space, and your personal bubble. You may find that it's easy to enforce and maintain these boundaries without fear of how people will react. You'll ruffle a lot of feathers and step on a lot of toes. People may start distancing themselves from you unless they have excellent communication, trust, and compassion. If you move through this, integration can help.

This isn't necessarily because you're antagonistic, adversarial, or competitive. It can come from love - love of yourself, love of humanity, and love of the planet. When your main motivation is the pursuit of the highest good for everyone, it will become incredibly easy and simple to stop tolerating things that create the opposite. It will matter too much to you to be silent.

Navigating this world and moving toward your dreams and goals can feel less like running a solo race with hurdles and obstacles, and more like choosing from a menu of delicious food at a big table with dear friends.

I just want you to understand the things that can start happening to you so they don't mess you up, freak you out, or scare you. The anger can be very frightening. Trust your body. Trust that the anger is there for a reason. If you can't name it, let it go. Just let it ride. Feel the anger, and give it a healthy outlet so it doesn't get stuck in your body. Therapists have really great ideas for addressing anger.

> Anger is not bad or wrong, and you're not bad or wrong for feeling it.

I hope that I haven't scared you off completely. My purpose in writing this book is to give you what I wish I'd had when I was where you are. While there were people around the world in small pockets using this, they weren't online with much of a following or using it in these ways for me to speak to or learn from.

We're headed somewhere with this. Eventually you won't need me to reassure you because you'll have the Mushroom Voice to say, "We love you. We've got you. Have faith. We're here to help. We love you. Hang in there."

Integration

Integration has become a buzzword in psychedelic circles recently and for a good reason. In microdoses and high doses, entheogenic medicine is so profound in what it does and how it works that it can cause such massive and sweeping changes in a short period of time that sometimes living with that can be difficult.

Trips can cause massive shifts in our view of reality. Microdoses can unearth deep trauma but can also cause changes in our bodies that we don't expect. Learning how to integrate this into how we live our daily lives can be challenging. How do we reconcile our new view of ourselves, the world, living things, and reality with our old belief system, especially when it all happened so quickly?

As of the writing of this book, there are very few therapists, psychologists, and doctors who work with these medicines. This is why integration coaches and specialists have emerged to fill that gap. Most of the time, they are not lettered after their names, nor do they attend schooling for counseling or therapy work. However, the field is growing, and slowly over time, we will have a large network of practitioners who have both used these medicines and are degreed, in addition to coaches and lower-key individuals who have an amazing capacity for helping others through these experiences.

That being said, there are a handful working with the Amanita muscaria mushroom. I am working to fill out a page of practitioners on my website as I can train them or find them and fully vet them. We are working in my MushroomVoice community with both an integration coach and a certified therapist who hosts Zoom meetings open to the community members and who also do private sessions. As the years roll on, I look forward to being an integral part of growing this database of practitioners.

I strongly encourage you to make sure that if, at any time, the use of this book or the Amanita becomes unsettling, please seek out professional help in integrating what you are learning and what might be happening as you progress. I was the first, and I had no one. I didn't seek help until high doses of psilocybin. There just wasn't anyone to help me, which is why I wrote this book. This book is basic help for integration at home on your own. It's a good helping hand for what to expect, so you won't be so surprised or worried. But if you experience the profound changes that are likely with the mushroom, go on and make a plan now for that event. Opening that vault from pre-birth to age six, or so can be deeply disturbing while also profoundly healing, and sometimes we just need help bridging that gap. I would say it took me about two years to make it through the most difficult parts of it. Once I added psilocybin, the integration began and was integral for me. I found that once I got past what I wrote about in this book, it was easier to explain to integration coaches.

Now that I have a few on tap who are familiar with using this mushroom, I offer their expertise to you, and I hope you will seek help with all of your integration, not just your path with this one entity. You can find help on AmanitaDreamer.Net

CHAPTER 8 — The Sentience of Fungi

When I first started using Amanita, I only believed in the current construct's definition of sentience. But five years of use of not only this mushroom but many others in high doses has brought me to an understanding that there are many different forms of sentience. Animal sentience is in the area of moving the physical; our abilities to move around the planet and affect the physical things with hands, paws, tails, tongues, and wings is only one form of manipulation of the environment. After using high-dose psilocybin and conversing with those entities, like almost everyone else who does the same, I learned of the sentience of plants and the wonderful lives of trees.

The Sentience of Trees

I began hearing the trees, learning my tree family locally, and understanding their personalities. They showed me another sentience and way of being on earth. For them, it isn't about movement and physicality; it's about chemistry and manipulating their environment with chemicals—accepting where they are and the things that go on around them that they can't control. The humans that come and go and never acknowledge them, theft of their resources, the deaths of their fellow tree family, the long slow process of death, watching their decay, living by roads, processing toxins, their conversations and lives with the bacteria and fungi, the conversations they have with other animals. Indeed they have very rich lives.

The concept that only humans can store information is simplistic.

There are many types of communication and many ways to store it and retrieve it. My concept of this for the fungi is that they use chemistry as the tools put forth by the mycelium into the fruiting bodies, but once they fruit, they are extensions of themselves, not just the reproductive parts. They are the extended ability to move above ground and, with the help of some animals, move around the planet. And they work by geometry. In the fruiting bodies is a geometry that, once finalized, moves energy. Written into it are instructions and information written by the mycelium. Those instructions are what to do with the onboard tools and the chemistry. And the only way it can be utilized is in tandem with another body's chemistry and energy. Together those geometries converse and set about utilizing the available tools of the chemistry available to both in unison. In this way, the fungi experience human existence, and humans experience fungal concepts and ideas, which is basically the ability to access information, movements, and abilities of other living things that one does not possess by birth.

The Sentience of Bees

The other concept that lends credence to fungal sentience is the sentience of animals and substances. I experienced this through mad honey. I took it on camera to be silly and just have an experience. What happened was, to this day, one of the top most profound experiences I have ever had. I entered the body of a bee and saw the world through its eyes. And the purpose for work and what drove that bee/me was a completely different way of experiencing the space-time continuum here. It was living in what felt to me like a very intense existence. I felt the shortness of life, even though most researchers believe that all living things experience their life spans as normal because they unfold at different rates of speed depending on how long the lifespan is.

But this life of this bee felt like it was known that life was short, but their existence made up for that by being very intense. The beingness was very much rooted in the ether, in light, and I hardly ever noticed the ground. I was acutely aware of the sky and the sun, but more importantly, it was the bliss I felt constantly. My buzzing created the bliss, and I could feel it echo out of me into the air. Flowers called to me, and the rich intensity of the craving and urge to go to them was all I could think of. Feeling the petals was another level of bliss, and I could feel nothing but love coming from the flower, and the embrace and communion between us was otherworldly and divine. I could hear music that was very familiar and similar to the universal hum I hear on high-dose psilocybin.

The information exchange with bees felt like creating physical energy with wings and creating a buzz and hum that was sustained. I felt like there was chemistry being created inside my body when I buzzed and that I would use the pollen created by both me and the flower with a signature unique to us both and that interaction that I would bring back to make honey with. The honey was the cumulative conversation of all the bees and flowers' conversations packed with universal sound, energy, and love with a recipe specific to earth at the time of collection.

The Sentience of Natural Phenomena

The trees and fungi both, separately, told me that lightning is sentient and that they feel like it is a deity; they get all star-struck about it. And yes, they fear it too. But the overarching theme of lightning is how exciting the possibility is that it will strike nearby, but in lower doses, like the electrical energy in a storm, it is medicine. I experienced the sentience of the wind while in Iceland, something completely surprising that I did not expect. And from there, the conversations with water and a raging river.

> To most humans reading this, this sounds insane and ridiculous. I know. I'm okay with that.

To those who study sacred geometry or Egyptian languages and geometry or who study cymatics and the nature of sound, or who study electrons, light, energy, waves or those who study particle physics, or those who study tree chemistry or plant chemistry and signaling hormones, any one single separate field would likely read this and say, well at least one piece of this is plausible. But if we could get all of these disciplines into one room, I feel certain about the conversation that would happen, even if none of them have ever used a tryptamine.

This is why we both fear and glorify fungi. The vast designs, ways they resemble and work like both plants and animals, how powerful their chemicals are, how complex the ways they seem to adapt and communicate and cause effects in their environments, and how easily one of them could kill us makes them fascinating. But I suggest that it is way more than that. I suggest it is written into our DNA, what we used to know as humans, and that is how we also used to understand and communicate in these ways. That the indigenous cultures still do and that our modern ideas of the simplicity of what we can measure and see as humans is all there is, is laughable.

I realize being public about the sentience of fungi and the Mushroom Voice has caused me to lose validity among those who think they are serious about fungi and who also fear losing the respect of their community. I believe the future will exonerate me in these respects, but I would rather further the cause of all living things here, build a bridge back to the conversations that need to exist, the respect across all living things, and what I believe will save the planet and humans' suffering, the unity again with the sacred here, than to keep respect among a community that fears its own emerging knowledge and allows that to inform their professional decisions.

When I talk to some of these people individually, they speak of the sentience of all the things like it's a normal conversation, which is cool. Those who work with fungi by ingesting them in higher doses have had these same conversations and experiences, and it's fun to talk to them about it. I feel much less alone among them. I feel like I live in a large family with my cats, the bees in my areas, the trees in my yard, and the plants here; we all wake up every day with greetings and hellos. I listen to how they view a day, the arc of the sun, the nightfall, the moon's phases, the encroaching seasonal changes, what they are concerned with, their outlooks on life, and what they fear and find joy in.

> *See, it's not just taking microdoses of mushrooms, and it's not just tripping; it's what those experiences open you to.*

From there, it's the experiences you have for months and years after that that make these conversations by ingestion of mushrooms so consciousness expanding. I have many people come at me who have never tripped trying to admonish me or folks who have never used muscarias saying, yeah but, and then try to compare their experiences with other fungi like all of them must be the same. This is so disrespectful to the fungi. It's like saying well, I met a skunk once, and based on that, I am pretty sure humans are the same.

I have been in science and lived it like a religion. I finally understand the role science plays for me now, and it is merely harm reduction. It is vital. Some parts of modern medicine are necessary, but the more pharma failed me and I was forced to find a natural alternative that was superior, the more I had the courage to keep leaping into the unknown. It has been a slow walk into the forest of understanding and out of the religion of modern concepts of isolating chemicals to measure them, isolating humans as the only intelligent beings, and believing that the only things true are what are measurable currently.

Like Alice, I drank the bottle and fell down the rabbit hole of the richness of the universal languages of geometry, sound, DNA, machine and living, wind, water, sun and earth sentience, electricity and energy, and the sum of the living things sentience's contributions to Universal Consciousness. And I'm okay with that. I'm more comforted by it and joyful about its existence than anything humans have come up with.

Does this mean that you need to believe this? Are you going to become a woo person who drank the potion? Not at all. What you believe has nothing to do with the power of healing in this medicine. And no one can tell you what your relationship to this medicine should be.

That is yours alone.

The Rest of This Book

From here, the rest of this book will cover the main lessons I and others have learned personally from our time spent with what I've come to call the Mushroom Voice. These are all concepts that I will hope to make clear for you to understand in your headspace, but your own journey with this mushroom will take you to places where you'll find yourself thinking, "Oh, now I understand what she was talking about!" because you'll be experiencing them yourself.

Each chapter will take a concept and go deeply into it. You may find glimpses of each of these things near the beginning of your protocol. Everyone experiences these "a-ha" moments in a unique order, each in its own timing. We are all different.

You can glimpse these in small ways near the beginning, in deeper ways the longer you dose or the higher you dose, and over time these changes can seat deeper. You will get better at learning how to use the information, how to harness the power in it, and how to work together with the Mushroom Voice and your own internal biology as tools for power, growth, and transformation.

PART 2
Down the Rabbit Hole

CHAPTER 9 — *Fear & Exhaustion*

One of the first things Amanita showed me is that my anxiety was tied to time (which isn't what you think it is–more on that later), my perceptions of reality, and my circadian rhythm–the speed of my living and my inner body.

They showed me by doing. I began to feel my mind shift in how it was making sense of my experiences, creating a lot more "a-ha" moments where I was connecting dots I hadn't connected before. Eventually, those connections started to connect to each other, which caused my body to behave differently, which in turn created more "a-ha's" from more connections.

I realized that literally everything is connected, to the point where I couldn't isolate any one thing as the cause of my anxiety. The answer is that everything was causing it, and for the first time, I'd found something that actually started reducing it. But it didn't stop there. The Mushroom Voice said,

*"It's not just **your** anxiety. This is **everyone's** anxiety.* Everyone's anxiety is both the cause and effect of everyone else's anxiety. It's why your societies are broken. It's why your lands are broken. It's why the humans are broken. It's why they are breaking the earth."

What would it look like if everyone's anxiety was your anxiety, and vice versa? It might look like someone feeling anxious about getting to work on time, so they cut you off on your morning commute, so you either go outward and fixate on how much of a jerk they are, go inward and wonder why everyone on the road is out to get you, or both. Now their anxiety has become your anxiety, and you're likely to either pay it forward and keep it in circulation, or incorporate it into how you experience yourself, damaging your self-image and capacity for self-love in the process.

The alarm goes off, you didn't get enough sleep. You've got to do this, someone needs you to do that, and this other thing urgently needs to be addressed before you can tackle that other thing. Before you know it, you're walking through your house with your toothbrush in your hand, your uneaten breakfast on the counter, and your brain having a mile-a-minute conversation with other people. Your nervous system is tipping you off that you have fears, and you have a narrative that those fears must drive your actions.

> Just as pain is the alarm system for your physical body, anxiety is the alarm system for your emotional body.

In the same way that pain has different levels of intensity and ways of expressing itself, so it is with anxiety. And, just like with most injuries that require recovery time, the more you neglect and ignore it, the louder it gets. Unless you've gone to great lengths to do the difficult, uncomfortable, and sometimes downright painful work of processing your anxiety and its sources within you, you likely have anxiety simply because you live in our current social environment.

Amanita can help to show you what you've been tolerating and help make the necessary changes. It means setting healthy boundaries and working through unhealthy ones. It means making people unhappy and uncomfortable with your existence, and it means being asked to make some pretty hard decisions. I hope you find help to do this with the power of the amanita and your health professional.

It's a tough road, but it's worth it, and once you start, the only way out is through. By dosing Amanita, you're going down the rabbit hole and you won't be coming back this way again. You won't be able to unlearn the things it's going to teach you. You'll start living the way we were meant to live. The societal structures and social systems we've created for ourselves really are antithetical to our highest good as a species. Our ancestors would look at us today and think, "Man, this is inhumane."

So, when you experience difficult things, it's not your body hating you; it's your body loving you. It's trying to get your attention. You wouldn't begrudge your body for sending pain signals if you smashed your thumb with a hammer, would you? So don't begrudge your body for experiencing anxiousness, ruminating thoughts, irritability, and confusion. Consider that perhaps all the things you have to do to be considered "functional" could be the very things causing your anxiety in the first place!

Fear

Do you generally move really quickly or pretty slowly?

Is that contributing to your anxiety?

How do you react to others around you, clearly having anxiety and expressing it?

Please write the things that you are most worried about right now.

#1 Fear

Place a mark on the spectrum where you feel each of these issues affects you.

	NEVER - NOT VERY NOTICEABLE							ALWAYS - VERY INTENSE
EXAMPLE (any mark will do)	⊖	·	·	·	·	♡	·	⊕
I get agitated easily	⊖	·	·	·	·	·	·	⊕
I have trouble falling and staying asleep	⊖	·	·	·	·	·	·	⊕
I have intrusive thoughts	⊖	·	·	·	·	·	·	⊕
I can't stop thinking about everything	⊖	·	·	·	·	·	·	⊕
I rush a lot and feel like I don't have time	⊖	·	·	·	·	·	·	⊕
I feel like times are worse than ever	⊖	·	·	·	·	·	·	⊕
I feel like I can't get ahead	⊖	·	·	·	·	·	·	⊕
I feel like my money will disappear	⊖	·	·	·	·	·	·	⊕
I'm afraid to go to bed	⊖	·	·	·	·	·	·	⊕
People drive crazy / traffic is bad	⊖	·	·	·	·	·	·	⊕
The internet is a shit show	⊖	·	·	·	·	·	·	⊕
People are generally mean	⊖	·	·	·	·	·	·	⊕
I can't get what I need at stores	⊖	·	·	·	·	·	·	⊕
I gain weight no matter what	⊖	·	·	·	·	·	·	⊕
I can't gain weight no matter what	⊖	·	·	·	·	·	·	⊕
I don't want to eat	⊖	·	·	·	·	·	·	⊕
I hate when people touch me	⊖	·	·	·	·	·	·	⊕
I get upset at the stupidity online	⊖	·	·	·	·	·	·	⊕
My memory is terrible	⊖	·	·	·	·	·	·	⊕
I don't do anything fun	⊖	·	·	·	·	·	·	⊕

Fatigue and Energetic Debt

The way your body functions biologically is to constantly meter out the energy it spends. Conserving energy is always its number-one priority. When it has the option for any chemical process, it will choose the least energy-expensive route. This is true for everything that happens in your body, from the way your hair grows and how you digest your food to how you break apart molecules and reuse proteins and how you kill a virus. It's also true for how your brain processes emotional information and where it's storing it in your body.

So, say you've got these normal, efficient processes and you're working, moving, and breathing. You've got energy moving through your body, keeping you going. You're being a good human with empathy and compassion and generosity. And you've got trauma stored here where you were grabbed, and there where you were in an accident, and you've got trauma stored in these places where you were told to shut up and be small. And then you've got trauma stored here where you were betrayed. And there where you got your heart broken. And all of this is in your body while it's just trying to move through the world and get stuff done.

Being as efficient as possible, your body detours the energy around that trauma, redirecting traffic this way and splitting it up that way to get it to where it needs to go. Unlike when you were young and your life force energy moved freely through you, now you're spending the bulk of your effort finding alternate routes around the stored trauma in your body and brain. No wonder you're so tired all the time. No wonder you burn through a day's worth of energy by 10:00 AM and need three cups of coffee to get through the rest of it. When you're out of energy and you take measures to keep on kicking anyway–slamming energy drinks, smacking yourself around, or just using sheer force of will to keep plugging away–you will pay the price for it later.

> You can borrow the energy from your future self, but you're racking up an energetic debt and you'll pay for it with interest.

When you go-go-go all day until you crash, you're giving your body and mind a lot of recovery work to do and not a lot of time to do it. The amount of stress you've put yourself through almost guarantees low-quality sleep, so you'll wake up the next morning having already spent 20% of that day's energy in your sleep. But you'll get up anyway, get ready, and do it all over again, hitting the same wall at 10:00 AM. So you'll borrow until you crash, then get unrestful sleep, wake up, go go go, crash. Borrow. Crash. Repeat. You keep doing this and you'll wind up somewhere, and that somewhere is hopeless exhaustion.

WORK SHEET #2

Exhaustion

Can you shift into a place of loving what your body is telling you?

Do you think you have negative talk to yourself about your energy levels?

When was the last time you felt like you had good, sustainable energy all day?

When our exhaustion is not responding to measures from outside, our body has borrowed so much energy that it is depleted. And once you've gotten that far, you'll feel like you're the problem because normal things aren't working to fix it. While mineral deficiencies are common among people with mental health issues and should be looked at, as well as sleep and other lifestyle and choices, , Amanita is a wonderful thing to experience.

#2 Exhaustion

- I feel like it's hopeless
- I have trouble falling and staying asleep
- I'm so tired all the time
- I think people don't like me
- I don't know what I want to do
- I feel like I'm never going to heal
- I feel like I can't get ahead
- I don't care if life passes me by
- I always let people down
- I force myself to get up
- I'm ugly
- Nothing works to make me feel better
- I think I have a disease
- I can't stop eating
- I don't want to eat
- If I had more money, I'd be okay
- Everything online is boring
- My memory is terrible
- I don't do anything fun

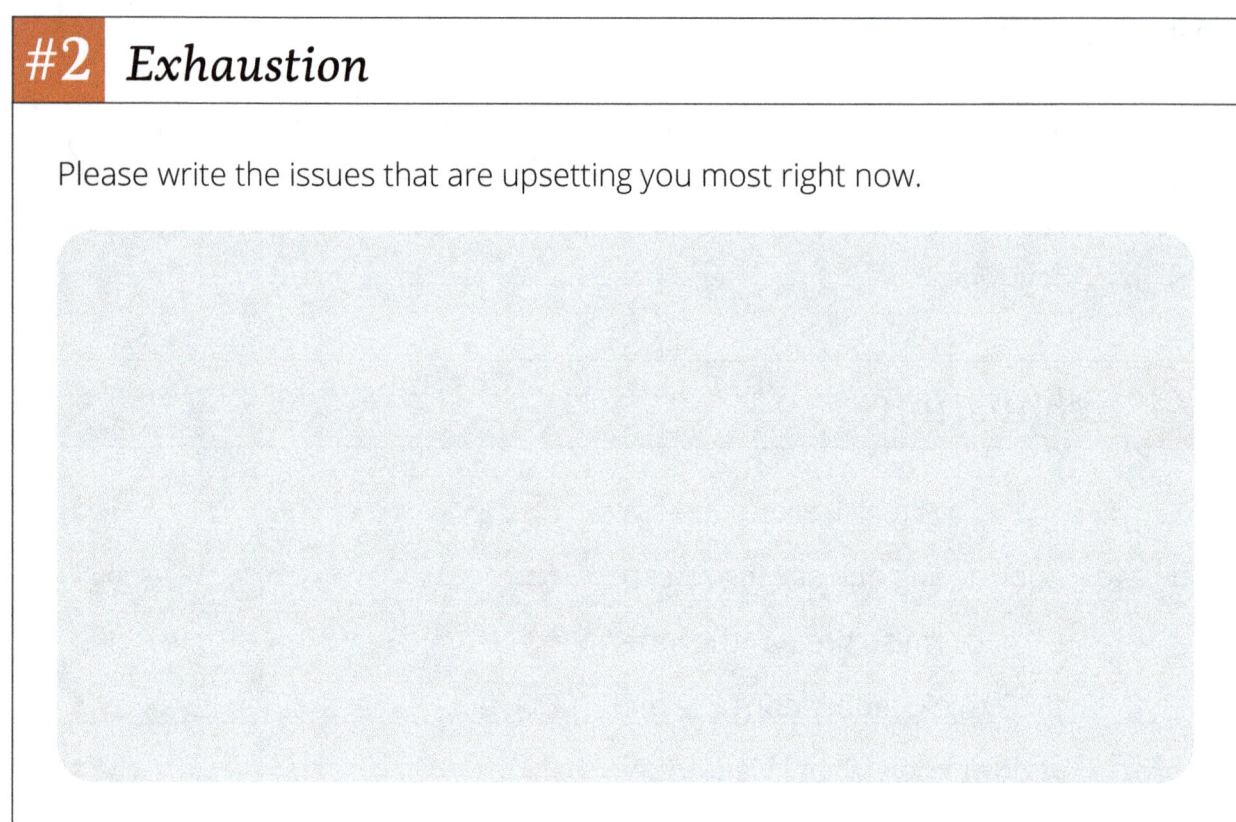

Your Body Loving You

You are light. Your cells are light. Remember from chemistry that atoms are the building blocks of everything on the periodic table of elements. Two hydrogen atoms and one oxygen atom bond together to make a water molecule.

An atom is composed of a cluster of protons and neutrons, called a nucleus, surrounded by a field of moving electrons, which are made of light. They behave like light, which has no mass, yet they behave like they have mass. They travel in waves like water and sound, yet they also seem to travel as individual particles moving in straight lines. They move up and down energy levels and bond with each other, and when observed, collapse into a single point of being. And if you get them too close to each other, they entangle and spin in opposite directions. They can bilocate and be in two places at once. They dip in and out of existence constantly. This describes every single electron in every single atom in your body.

I believe electrons are the God Particle in us. They are where the Divine meets our meat sack like some infinitesimally small energy bridge. Yes, they are the building blocks to the building blocks to the building blocks to all life on earth, which has to follow earth-based rules. When I have taken high doses of psilocybin, I have witnessed the actual light and geometrical bridge of this in vivid, living, breathing, pulsing color.

By consciousness, spiritual, energetic design based on using high doses of mushrooms, I believe that by the time we experience their end product, it feels like tangible, dense, breakable skin and bones. But those light particles create atoms, which create molecules, which create chemicals, which create cells, which create you.

So, in a very real way, you are literally light.

And light is the tangible expression of love. It is in your body's very nature to love you every minute of every day.

When we live exhausted by energy depletion or anxiety, depleted minerals, and sleep debt, we may have some issues we may not be able to pinpoint. While they can be attributed to some other issues, together with exhaustion and anxiety, they can create symptoms that the Amanita muscaria mushroom seems to be very good at changing in profound ways. To get a baseline on how you are now, for your future self and the activities here, please answer the following questions.

#3 *Energy Levels*

Please write here, the fears you have and what you really miss.

WORKSHEET #3: Energy Levels

I get tired not long after I wake up ⊖ · · · · · · · · ⊕
I don't have motivation to do my work ⊖ · · · · · · · · ⊕
I have random odd thoughts ⊖ · · · · · · · · ⊕
I can't think deeply or for long ⊖ · · · · · · · · ⊕
I move slowly like I'm in mud ⊖ · · · · · · · · ⊕
I feel like I'll never have energy ⊖ · · · · · · · · ⊕
I want to just stay in bed ⊖ · · · · · · · · ⊕
I want people to leave me alone ⊖ · · · · · · · · ⊕
I order food most of the time ⊖ · · · · · · · · ⊕
I resent the people I take care of ⊖ · · · · · · · · ⊕
I'm so out of shape ⊖ · · · · · · · · ⊕
I have odd symptoms like I'm sick ⊖ · · · · · · · · ⊕
Everything hurts ⊖ · · · · · · · · ⊕
I don't like brushing my teeth ⊖ · · · · · · · · ⊕
I can't do laundry or dishes ⊖ · · · · · · · · ⊕
I don't respond to messages ⊖ · · · · · · · · ⊕
I hate when people invite me to things ⊖ · · · · · · · · ⊕
I don't care how I look these days ⊖ · · · · · · · · ⊕
My memory is terrible ⊖ · · · · · · · · ⊕
I'm always late ⊖ · · · · · · · · ⊕

CHAPTER 10 — *Sleep*

Amanita is the love mushroom, the ego mushroom, the flow mushroom, the balance-of-opposites mushroom, and the power mushroom. As you might have guessed, it's also the sleep mushroom. This is an important thing to understand and incorporate. Why do you think, of all the names I could've gone with, I go by Dreamer?

> Of all the things this mushroom is known for, it is known for how it affects your sleep.

There are no studies as of the writing of this book to support what I am about to say here. I hope to engage in some studies on these things soon, and you can watch AmanitaDreamer.net for updates as I do. Since this mushroom helps with core memories and issues from pre-birth to age six or when that development window closes, the work is often done in sleep or in what we think is sleep. I believe that while this mushroom can heal us in Theta, the phase of sleep where a lot of physical healing happens, I also believe it is working on those core issues in our sleep. Therapy seeks to reach this core, hypnosis, EMDR; these therapies are trying to help find the root of triggers and issues in this place. I believe that in our deep sleep in Theta, REM, and Delta, is when much of this is unearthed, rearranged, cleaved, fixed, and healed. I also believe that for a lot of it, we are actually conscious and awake. This is the "trip" phase of the experience. We drift in and out of awareness, leave our bodies, and travel and return in and out, depending on the dose we take. Again there is nothing in science substantiating this.

Your sleep may change in many ways. You might experience restlessness, wakefulness, odd sleeping patterns, fatigue in the morning, energy in the morning, hard days full of memories, and good days full of hopefulness.

Please allow sleep to do what sleep needs to do for you.

> Some mornings, you will wake up feeling really dull and thick in the head, and that means the muscimol was doing its job overnight. It will wear off throughout the day.

> On other mornings, you'll wake up super early and be ready to go, even if you're not normally a morning person. Go ahead and start your day - that's the ibotenic acid giving you a kick start.

> Some nights, you'll get the most peaceful, restful sleep you've had in your entire life, even if you're the type who doesn't fall asleep easily and wakes up several times throughout the night.

> On other nights, you'll have the most visceral nightmares, waking up every 20 minutes and feeling absolutely terrified and traumatized the next morning to the point where you have to call in sick to work and spend the day hiding from the world. That just means the mushroom got busy doing what it needed to do.

And all of these ranges of effects are perfectly normal. This is the work. So don't judge the sleep you're getting (or not getting). If any of this lasts or is upsetting, please see your doctor.

Shaming yourself is not allowed. Nitpicking what you did or didn't do is not allowed. Just be present for the learning and be grateful for the times when you take it, and you just have this really cool, nice, beautiful experience. One of the reasons the mushroom works in this way is to get you to start paying more attention to your body. And like our waking life, our sleep life is just as important, and this is why you will see your sleep change so much. The more you pay attention to your body, the more of yourself you're able to love.

Having good sleep hygiene deeply affects your sleep. New studies show that if you go to bed at the same time each night, the first 2 hours of sleep will affect the rest of your sleep. Your body will start your sleep cycle at the same time each night with these 2 hours, and if you miss them and go to bed later, you won't sleep as well and can feel groggy the next day. Other things affect sleep too. Too much light in the room will keep you from going into deeper sleep. Temperature affects sleep. Proper body alignment, snoring, and blood sugar all affect sleep.

WORKSHEET #4: Sleep

- I struggle to fall asleep ⊖ — — — — — — — — ⊕
- I have delayed sleep times ⊖ — — — — — — — — ⊕
- I wake up constantly all night ⊖ — — — — — — — — ⊕
- I don't start deep sleep until the morning ⊖ — — — — — — — — ⊕
- I have night terrors and bad dreams ⊖ — — — — — — — — ⊕
- I get anxious at night ⊖ — — — — — — — — ⊕
- I wait until I am falling asleep to go to bed ⊖ — — — — — — — — ⊕
- I feel unrested every morning ⊖ — — — — — — — — ⊕
- I'm afraid to go to bed ⊖ — — — — — — — — ⊕
- I wake up wanting to stay in bed ⊖ — — — — — — — — ⊕
- I can't get comfortable in my sleep ⊖ — — — — — — — — ⊕
- I don't remember dreaming ⊖ — — — — — — — — ⊕
- I know I dream, but I don't remember ⊖ — — — — — — — — ⊕
- I am a restless sleeper ⊖ — — — — — — — — ⊕
- I have bad things happen in my sleep ⊖ — — — — — — — — ⊕
- I don't have any kind of regular routine ⊖ — — — — — — — — ⊕
- I sleep with a light on ⊖ — — — — — — — — ⊕

#4 Sleep

Please write the parts about sleep that you are most disturbed by right now.

One of the things Amanita will do is make you start to love and value your sleep. Prepare to start investing in making your bedroom and your bed your most holy of places. Start thinking about looking for the best pillow for your sleep and how you sleep. Spend time learning about how temperature affects sleep. Studies show that the best temperature for humans to actually get the best sleep is 16-19C or 60 - 67F. Watch as your needs change for sound, like white or green noise. Do you need air circulating? Start to save for a mattress that supports you for better sleep. Invest in sheets that are actually comfortable and fit properly and move correctly with how you sleep. This process can take several years, approaching one item at a time, but this mushroom will show you how truly important your sleep is in your mental and physical health.

You will be doing more work on sleep in this healing than you have done, probably ever. Maybe your sleeping arrangements with a partner need some drastic changes, potentially separate beds in the same room or separate rooms. Maybe your child that wakes you up a lot needs to be in the room with you so both can sleep through the night. Maybe they are afraid and need you close by. Maybe the room itself is just not a great sleeping room, and the family room needs to become the sleeping room.

Maybe by now, you are learning convention, society, and norms might not be the best guide for each of us, for what works best or for how we live our lives. Sleep will be yet another area where you will be challenged to allow, change, and prioritize yourself and your health.

CHAPTER 11

Time - Part 1

There's this idea that we're all moving through time in the same direction and at the same speed. Society needs this idea. It depends on it. Can you imagine a world where meeting up at 2:15 on a Tuesday afternoon meant something different to you than it did to me? On some level, any functioning human society needs time to be universal and uniform, so for the sake of society, we've made time universal and uniform. And this version of time is what I call "government time."

And also, it's not real.

You think time is outside of you, like you're swimming through a river, and time is the water you're swimming in and the current that's pulling you in a specific direction. One of the first things that Amanita is going to teach you is that time only exists inside you. It actually doesn't exist outside of you at all. You're not moving through time; *you ARE time.*

Your essential self, your consciousness (your soul, your Buddha nature, whatever you want to call it), exists outside of time. It experiences every moment simultaneously, much like how you can look at a ruler and see every inch marker at once. Imagine your life from birth to death is a deck of cards, and each experience you have is a single card in that deck. In order to make any kind of meaning from that life, you'd need to sort them into some kind of order. Time is what we create to put our cards in order. It's much easier to make sense of our experiences when we have birth on one side and death on the other, and everything in between is organized according to their distance from those two fixed points. Time is an organizational tool our consciousness creates to bring order to what would otherwise be a chaotic cacophony of experiences.

As everyone operates uniquely, everyone creates time uniquely. How high-strung we are, stressed and exhausted we are, and how we cope with that can make us speed up how we work and move. It can make us slow down, like walking through mud, and processing more slowly. How we create time for ourselves determines how quickly we speak, how quickly we walk, how quickly we comprehend, how fast or slow a video seems to us, how we view and record time, and how we recall and remember time. How you create time will shape how you move through the world. How well your way of moving through the world fits (or doesn't fit) within society's expectations will determine how much anxiety and/or depression you experience. Anxiety causes your speed and energy expenditure, which can clash with society and cause more anxiety and exhaustion.

Government time isn't bad or wrong; it's just not real. You are time, and time is you. And your best case scenario will always be the one in which you find a way to move through this world according to your own internal time/speed/energy expenditure.

Rushing is Violence

The first assignment I have for you is this:

I don't mean not moving quickly. If you're a runner and you're competing in a race, then you are moving quickly with purpose and maybe enjoyment or focus. If you are happy and running toward the love of your life as they get off the train, that's full of love and goodness.

> **NO. MORE. RUSHING.**

There's moving quickly with good reason, and there's *rushing*. You know, when you've planned your vacation and everything is in order, but the babysitter's late, so you won't leave for the airport as early as you were expecting, and your maps app is telling you there was just a wreck on the freeway so it's all backed up, and now you're *rushing* to get out the door as soon as possible. You're *rushing* through traffic to get to the airport, and when you get there, you'll *rush* to get through security and find your gate in time.

This is the rushing we won't be doing anymore. It's mentally rushing. It's emotionally violent. When you operate from this space, you are seriously damaging yourself, and that's got to stop immediately if you want to truly heal.

Nothing is worth the toll inflicted on your nervous system when you rush.

Nothing.

> Does this mean you can't drive faster to get to the store because you know that you've got five things to get and you gotta be somewhere in ten minutes?

> *Absolutely. This means you cannot do that anymore.*

Instead, you'll need to learn how to shift into accepting what this will mean. In this case, you'll be late. That's it. You'll need to start getting used to being unapologetically late. If you need to let people know, then you need to let people know. Instead of driving dangerously to shave a couple minutes off your time, simply communicate openly, take responsibility for the decisions you made that caused you to be late, renegotiate agreements if necessary, and then come back to the present and be with yourself.

No one else's problem needs to become your emergency.

Rushing is insisting that where you are in this present moment is wrong - something to be fixed or escaped. Rushing is trying to lasso the future and yank it into the present before its time. All we have is the present, so rushing is a rejection of all that is. No wonder our bodies respond with stress and anxiety! Our bodies are here and now!

The question to ask yourself in these moments is, why are you so afraid of being late? Are they going to yell at you? Are you afraid they're not going to like you? Are you averse to a narrative that you don't respect other people's time? Why does that scare you? What makes their time so important that it's worth dishonoring yours? Or are you

> **DISCLAIMER**
> There will always be extenuating circumstances, and there are times when rushing is the best answer. Those times are few and far between, and the problem comes when we rush over the small things as though they're the big things. One thing Amanita helps us understand is that 99% of them are small things. There's almost never a good reason to rush.

actually worried that no one will care because, deep down, you fear your presence isn't valued or even noticed? What is the thing behind the thing?

> *These are the types of conversations you'll find the Amanita asking you to have with yourself.*

If you're late because you just don't care about other people's experiences, you'll have to have that conversation with yourself and figure out how to grow some empathy. If you're chronically late because you have ADHD and you don't really flip on until the 11th hour, then you'll have to have conversations with yourself about better planning strategies and maybe develop some discipline around utilizing executive function tools like reminders and calendar appointments. Whatever the reasons for the lateness, you will be asked by the Amanita, to find them.

What about the people who are harsh with you, who will judge you? Are those the kinds of people you need to be dealing with? Is it an option to deal with someone else? If not, proactively create space for open, honest, responsible communication about not just that you're late, but why you're late, and how you can support each other to make both of your time scales work more harmoniously together.

Are you, like I was, rushing to get things done in the hopes of crossing off your to-do list, hoping that today is the day you complete it? Or that you can finish all the things in time to have some downtime before bed? I had to learn how to be able to deeply rest and do nothing while incomplete tasks stay waiting. That's a lot to unpack too.

Putting this no-rushing policy into practice will shift you to a place where you're living in flow, acceptance, and grace. Yes, you can meditate daily for years, start a yoga practice, learn breathwork techniques, and cull your commitments to make more breathing room in your schedule. Those will all get you there eventually. Through my relationship with Amanita, I've found that simply choosing to abide strictly by this one rule is the single most efficient and sustainable way to achieve and maintain this state of surrender and flow where your body can actually function the way it's meant to. Eventually, it will become your normal state of existence, just as it was before our society got its hands on you and insisted that you rush to keep up with its inhumane demands. It's not uncommon to see a parent of a toddler saying, "Hurry up!"
And indeed, in my travels, meeting up with hosts and co-workers in the spiritual space

with years of experience in yoga and breathwork and meditation, they STILL rushed, and I had to ask them to please calm/slow down. I refuse to "keep up" with people. It's the one thing I have encountered more than any other thing in my travels.

WORKSHEET #5: Perceptions of Time

Statement	− ←→ +
Life drags on slowly	⊖ · · · · · · · ⊕
Things always happen to take my time	⊖ · · · · · · · ⊕
I don't have time to complete my tasks	⊖ · · · · · · · ⊕
I have to rush a lot	⊖ · · · · · · · ⊕
If I rush people, they will respond	⊖ · · · · · · · ⊕
People are unreliable	⊖ · · · · · · · ⊕
Things rarely work out as planned	⊖ · · · · · · · ⊕
It's important to know what day it is	⊖ · · · · · · · ⊕
Holidays are important	⊖ · · · · · · · ⊕
Jan 1 helps mark time and is important	⊖ · · · · · · · ⊕
Without exact time society would collapse	⊖ · · · · · · · ⊕
Time creates order	⊖ · · · · · · · ⊕
Every day has the same amount of time	⊖ · · · · · · · ⊕
Time is speeding up	⊖ · · · · · · · ⊕
Good times go faster	⊖ · · · · · · · ⊕
I spend my time wishing for time off	⊖ · · · · · · · ⊕
People should work more efficiently	⊖ · · · · · · · ⊕
I have to know what time it is all the time	⊖ · · · · · · · ⊕
Changes to my schedule are hard for me	⊖ · · · · · · · ⊕
I wish I didn't have responsibilities	⊖ · · · · · · · ⊕

#5 Perceptions of Time

Please write here what you would do without any responsibilities.

One cool thing that happens when you start dropping into your body and living through that place of surrender and presence is that you'll start recognizing other people doing it too. You may find yourself breathing a little more slowly, moving a little more intentionally, being a little more graceful, accepting what is, and allowing things to be what they are instead of fighting to control them.

This doesn't seem to have anything to do with time. I totally understand that. The Amanita will show you differently. When you start flowing and accepting what is, you'll see people. When you walk up to them, you'll see them, and I mean *really* see them. You'll know it. You'll recognize it even if you've never met them before. This is a common theme among things you'll learn from any mycelial beings, simply because mycelial beings are networks incarnate. They're connective by nature, so as you build relationships with them, you'll become more connected yourself, and you'll start to see yourself in others as you slowly come to realize we're all one single organism.

You will begin to connect many dots about how time is connected to every single aspect of your life, stress, and rigidity. Amanita will help ease you into some transitions with respect to time, energy, exhaustion, plans, order, allowing, flowing, and anxiety.

Please do this exercise:

> Get an empty glass and set it on the counter. Think about getting it filled with water as fast as possible knowing that if you don't, you will be punished. Pretend it's urgent. RUSH and fill it and put it in the refrigerator quickly!!!
> GO GO GO GO!
>
> Okay, now get the glass and empty it and return it to its original place. This time, I want you to also get it filled as quickly as you can and put it in the fridge. But this time I want you to work hard to keep thoughts out, to not speak voices and meaning to yourself. There is no punishment and no rewards. Just quick purposeful movement. I want you to work to remain very calm inside your body, in your mind, in your core. Ready? Go!

If you can't do this or feel it, continue to practice this in your daily life. Try to embody what it feels like to rush versus what it feels like to move quickly with centered calmness. When you find yourself rushing, do this:

Slow down immediately and think about whether or not this speed is necessary. If it is necessary that you move quickly, center and calm yourself while you do.

Remember rushing is emotionally violent, causes suffering, and is not a necessary part of life.

CHAPTER 12 — Ritual vs. Rigidity

If you identify as a somewhat functioning adult, you likely have habits, routines, and rituals you've set up for yourself that you believe make your life more efficient and less stressful. You may think this structure has nothing to do with your anxiety. You may think it's actually a really good thing. You may be very proud of yourself for the structure you've built to keep your life moving along without anything falling through the cracks. And you should be! It likely took years of self-discovery and trial and error, and boatloads of willpower and determination. Also,

there's a very thin line here between a healthy habit and a fear-based desire.

One of the first things that Amanita is going to do is dislodge you from that.

It may be a little frightening the first time you go to one of your routines and instead of thinking, "This is good. I need to do this. My executive function depends on it," you think, "Ew. If this is something I need to do, why does it feel ew?" That may be the first little hint. Or you may just accidentally skip it altogether because you forgot and then panic when you realize you actually have to try to care about doing it, or it won't get done. Or maybe you'll realize you never really needed to do it in the first place and laugh at how often that's the case. We are not addressing an OCD disorder here, but just rigidity.

Rigidity

If you've really been suffering from chaos or unpredictability or anxiety, you can habit yourself into a position of rigidity. Amanita is a mushroom of flow and openness. It is going to shake you loose from your rigidity because rigidity will get you into black-and-white thinking (we'll talk about that more in-depth later). This light must always be turned off. I must do the dishes every night and wipe the counter every time I do the dishes. I must always check my email or always do this, or always do that. If you're doing enough of these, rigidity becomes your comfort zone, and it becomes incredibly easy to immediately say "no" to anything that doesn't fit within the parameters of the life you've made for yourself. What happens when gifts come your way? Opportunities? If your sense of security is grounded in the fact that you check the mail first thing in the morning, the stool gets stored by the sink, Tuesday nights are bingo nights, laundry day is Thursday, and I walk my dog on this path every morning and that path every evening, then anything that might throw a kink in your system will be met with an immediate "no" because you'll see it as something that would destroy your system when really, it might just be the thing that could liberate you from it.

You lock yourself into your own misfortune and your own victimhood. These are all based on fear, and that fear comes from your inability to trust yourself to solve a problem or rise to the occasion when that shows up. You've outsourced your decisioning power to a system of your own design because you don't trust yourself to make those decisions on your own.

Chances are, that's because you've been actively silenced. Only in recent generations are parents starting to believe their children are capable of governing their own worlds and that self-governance power will grow naturally as their worlds expand. Before, it was (and still is, in much of the world) commonplace for parents to assume children are incapable and incompetent. If you were treated that way as a child, you likely internalized that message, and on some level deep down, still believe you're incapable and/or incompetent without some kind of system to hold you in place and guide your next move.

This is how Amanita approaches these things. It breaks down the "if/then" structures we create from our rigid thinking. If you let Amanita do its work to dissolve those lines and turn your rigid thinking into flexible thinking, the whole world will open up to you.

Ritual

Amanita is the ritual mushroom. And a lot of times, we create compulsions because what we don't have in our lives is ritual. Some things just need to be done. You need to take out the trash to avoid a living space full of garbage. Maybe you have the compulsion to take it out at the same time on the same day every week, or maybe you just do it when it needs to be done. Rituals are like that. They're not unhealthy and rigid but rather practices that simply must be done to live a life free of anxiety and chaos.

One of the things that Amanita is going to cause in you is this craving for ritual. One of the interesting ways that I've seen this is when people want to create a ritual around Amanita because Amanita is at the epicenter of everything, making their lives better. This makes sense at first until you realize this is similar to someone pointing at the moon to show you its brilliance, and instead of looking at what they're pointing at, you focus on the finger they're using to point. If you want to make a ritual out of taking your Amanita, loving the Amanita, worshiping your Amanita, drying your Amanita, storing your Amanita, etc., do that. Nobody's stopping you, and that's beautiful. What I want to bring to your attention is that through the use of Amanita, the hope for you is that you will dislodge your compulsions and let them all go. The mushroom isn't going to point to certain things and say, "This is good, that's bad, this is the right thing to do, that's the wrong thing to do." What it's going to do is bring your attention to certain things and give you a lens to see them through so you can assess for yourself if they're necessary things for your well-being, or fear-based things that were programmed into you. Ritualizing your relationship with Amanita could be the best way for you to interact with it, or it could be you just migrating your compulsions from "bad" stuff to "good" stuff. Only you can know.

Humans have had rituals for thousands of years. It is a practice that creates magic, safety, and mental health. We cannot separate our health from ritual, and ritualistic practices will naturally begin to unfold in your life as the mushroom voice enters your world. When you begin to feel the need for ritual, allow it to unfold in your world and adapt your existing rituals, compulsions, and habits to it.

 *Daily Ritual*

The first thing I want you to do is to find a daily ritual and preferably put it at the time of day that you find the most difficult to handle. If it's waking up first thing in the morning, then let's find a beautiful ritual for right when you wake up. I have a meditation book, and maybe reading a meditation with your morning drink with some Amanita cold water extract is a new ritual. Maybe it's two in the afternoon when you hit that slump, and you have a lot of shame around the fact that you need to be productive, but all you want to do is take a nap. Maybe it's 5:00 because you had abusive parents or a partner, and you lived in fear for when they came home, and that nervous system alarm still goes off around that time. Maybe it's right before bed because that's when you start reviewing your day, and all you can think about are things you regret or what you fear moving forward. Choose a time of day that challenges you the most.

> The first ritual we are going to introduce is tea.

For most of my life, the sacredness of tea was lost on me. I know the Brits have tea time. I know the Japanese and Chinese love their tea. But I never quite understood it until Amanita showed me and taught me the importance of tea.

But because of this particular time on earth and the definition of medicine, a lot of us are very disconnected from what living medicine and healing are, and how humans on earth have been using medicine for thousands of years. Our medicine came to us in the form of a warm tea, and it came to us from a human being who intimately knows us and genuinely cares for our well-being–someone who knows of our medical history and our family and intimately works with the land and the medicines that are in the tea that they're bringing to us.

And they learned from their predecessor–a mentor under whom they've apprenticed their whole life–not just eight years of medical school. They started apprenticing very young, walking the fields and forests with this person, learning about the earth by first feeling it under their feet. They can probably remember being very young and the sun coming up and this beautiful, wise healer they look up to saying, "Feel the leaf. Do you see how it's soft on top and shiny underneath? This is the one we want. Can you get eight of those, please?" And they have memories of the breathtaking sunrise, the smell of the spring air, the love of this human, and feeling the energy of that plant. This person taught them how to ask for the plant's permission and how to work with the land, and know when to take from that plant and when not to take from that plant while they had their bare feet on the ground. They watched that plant go through all of its seasons year after year. They know the medicine as a sentient living being.

They know how to harvest it. They know how to dry it. They keep it in containers that are valuable to them and that have been gifted to them by other members of the community. When they go to use the medicine, they're using their intuition and their heart when they know five medicines can help your symptoms right now, and they use their energy to know which of those five to pull and in what amounts. Because at that moment, it's the wisdom of the medicine guiding them—not a prescription, not a one-size-fits-all. As they're pulling it, they're talking to the medicine, they're having conversations with it on your behalf, and as they put it in the cup with love and they get that water, and they pour it, they're smelling it, and they're feeling it, and they're saying, "Nope, it's missing something. Of course." And then they go get the one other thing, and they add it, and then they know when it's right. They are literally bringing millions of voices to that moment–voices of their ancestors and their ancestors and theirs, and also of the predecessors and the genetic beings that lived for thousands of years to this plant and all of these things that are in this medicine. And when you've got seven medicines in a cup going back thousands of years to all of their ancestors, plus your healer's ancestors, there are so many voices in this, so that when they bring it to you and hand it to you, you feel it. You know what's coming to you when you look up to take it from them. The energy and the power that's coming across as you take it from their hand and you smell it, you feel it as you drink it in.

This is living medicine.

The energy and power and the healing in that alone–the intention that's being carried, the fact that you know you deserve this, and that you're being healed with love–is much more than the placebo effect. There is power in that intention. There's power in knowing you're being healed and in respect for the healer who's giving it to you. When you drink it, that's just the icing on the cake because you've already done most of the work in allowing it, and they've done most of the work in bringing that energy to you.

By the time you smell it and get those molecules into your bloodstream and then drink it, you're getting all that healing on board into all the cells in your body. Multiply that by all of your genetic ancestors times the thousands of years that we have been holding a warm cup of medicine, and you will understand the power of tea. Tea is not just tea. Tea is medicine, tea is life, and you know it. Your cells know it. Your body knows it. And if you start working with natural healing medicines, with that in mind, with intention, you may not have a healer giving it to you, but you can be that healer.

This is why I would like to ask you that your first daily ritual be a healing medicinal tea. Start with whatever you've got. If the only thing you can do is go to the store and get something like a yogi tea or some corporate name brand tea, that is still a medicinal tea. Eventually, you'll learn which herbs and natural ingredients are good for treating certain symptoms and conditions, and you'll be making your own tea from the earth in no time.

If you want to make it an evening tea, then you can do blue lotus, which stacks really well with Amanita, as do passion flower and chamomile. And then pour your dose of your Amanita in there and make that the ritual that you do at 6:00 or 7:00 at night. Especially if it gives you a little bit of energy and if you train the people around you to know that this is important to you, that will be the beginning of you truly setting some good boundaries around actually nurturing yourself. Remember to do it at whatever time of day is hardest for you. If it's first thing in the morning, then make it a stimulant tea. If it's 5:00 in the afternoon and you're not ready for Amanita yet, I just make a fruity tea and put a couple of calming things in there, like some blue lotus.

If you don't have a favorite mug, start putting your intentions on getting one that will be for this purpose. It's even better if it's handmade. It's even better if they made it specifically for you. Wherever you get your mug, that specific mug will be used only for this ritual. And once you grab that mug, I want you to take a moment to just center yourself, calm down, and bring yourself to this moment. Think through every movement as though it's its own mini ritual. Then take those herbs with intention and use your hands to sprinkle them in the water. Not inside a strainer or container, but throw those herbs right in that water. If you're using a teabag, tear it open and feel them as they move through your fingers and fall into the water. Add these things with intention and smell it and feel it and talk to it. Yes, talk to it. And then, when you pour the water in there, just watch what it does to the leaves and how they swirl around. Put your sweetener in there if you're using sweetener, and stir it all up.

While it steeps, turn the ringer down on your phone, turn it off completely, or put it in another room. Turn your monitor off. Or make sure you let people know you're going to be unavailable for the next ten minutes. Set that time aside. Something in the oven? Turn the oven off. And then sit and think about the triggers and the things that bother you about this time of day. Thank Amanita that we're going to be addressing this. Feel hopeful about this. Feel good about it. Be excited about the fact that we are going to eliminate this as a stressor in your daily life. And then go get the mug. Sit with it and smell it and feel the warmth of the mug. And then picture your ancestors. You are doing something millions of humans–billions of humans–have done in that moment. Take a sip, feel the warmth in your throat, and let it go down. This is the beginning of the healing.

If you have to go back to being busy after that, that's fine. Just those five minutes alone can be life-changing because you just did it with awareness. This is the start of creating your daily ritual. Once you have one daily ritual, I would like for you to start thinking about some other really small things you can add to your day. If you grew up being abused first thing in the morning, you might start your day by opening your curtains, looking at the trees, and thinking, "Look, no one's abusing me." Just whatever other times are difficult for you, wrap a ritual around them to make that time sacred and full of presence and gratitude.

 ## Weekly Ritual

Once you have some dailies, I also want you to start thinking about a weekly ritual. It can be whatever day of the week you hate the most. A lot of us are just programmed to hate Mondays. Others of us dread Fridays because we spend that day panicking, trying to get everything done before the weekend. Sometimes it's your day off because you get overwhelmed by all the things you need to do that you couldn't do while you were working. Maybe it's any day that you have to go to work. Maybe it's your first day back to work after you've had some days off. But pick whatever day is difficult for you and create a ritual for that day.

 ## Monthly Ritual

The monthly ritual is very important for helping us mark time and helping to ground us about the movement of larger periods of time. Finding what resonates with you personally is important. Marking the changing of the month may appeal to you. Maybe the middle of the month seems to drag on, and you could use a good ritual to break it up. I have a flag stand in my yard, and I change it, I have a mailbox wrap for each month, and I change out my hand towels and other linens in my house for each month. Some other examples are deep cleaning your house on the first of the month, journaling by candlelight on the last day of the month, or taking yourself on a date on the first weekend. I'm sure you can think of many other ideas. Whatever it is, pick something that's doable and doesn't require anyone else's participation (if they cancel, there goes your ritual). It needs to be something life-giving that you enjoy and look forward to. In the days leading up to it, you should be chomping at the bit to get to do your ritual. If you're thinking, "Ugh, in three days, I have to clean my whole house," then maybe consider picking a different monthly ritual. Timing a monthly ritual around the new moon or full moon can be a wonderful new practice.

 Quarterly Ritual

And then, of course, we have quarterly rituals. These go back thousands of years to when people celebrated solstices and equinoxes. This is ingrained in our DNA. If you've ever done an egg hunt on Easter or given gifts on Christmas, then you've celebrated equinoxes and solstices–or at least participated in festivities that were created to piggyback on pre-existing cultural celebrations of these events. So create your own. Find the solstices and equinoxes on your calendar and develop your own rituals for them or find celebrations of these events and make plans to attend them with others. It can be your own personal candlelight vigil to shed the old and make way for the new. Maybe a barefoot walk in the park where you ground and get in touch with nature. Maybe your ritual is turning off your phone and binge-watching your favorite movies. Or maybe you save up and travel to a ritual celebration provided by others for a three-day event.

> *Amanita will begin asking you for ritual and ceremony as it dislodges you from your rigidity and compulsive practices.*

The more you lean into it, the more you're going to see something very simple and beautiful start to happen: as you start letting go of rigidity and compulsion, you'll find yourself beginning to let go of other things too. You'll start to flow more with life, and be less rigid about how it's unfolding. If you're sitting in traffic and late to something, you won't panic like you used to – it'll feel so easy and natural to simply text whoever is waiting on you to let them know the situation and then turn on some music and enjoy the ride. When someone breaks an agreement with you, you'll find forgiveness and understanding are more accessible to you because you'll recognize your own humanity in them. Instead of feeling personally affronted when someone interrupts you, you might find yourself thinking, "If it's worth interrupting me for, then it must be super important to them. And they're important to me, so I want to hear what they have to say." These are shifts Amanita will be inviting you to make.

The Transition from Rigidity to Flow

The transition from rigidity to flow can be rocky. There's kind of a catch-22 that happens for a lot of people. Your compulsions and anxiety-backed rigid structures have been your safety net for years, maybe decades. And breaking free from them could feel unsafe like you're falling without a net to catch you. And out of sheer habit, what will you do? Default back to the very same rigid compulsions that have been making you feel safe this whole time. The only thing is, now you have Amanita, so returning to those old habits starts to feel gross to a lot of folks.

Amanita is the safety mushroom. The ritual and ceremony she's inviting you into will be your new safety net. This may seem like replacing familiar rigidity with new rigidity. The difference is your old compulsions are like scaffolding designed to stave off the anxiety that comes from participating in the chaos of our fear-based, panic-inducing society that runs on government time. The rituals the Amanita asks of you will be like markers in your life that will support and expand you so that you no longer feel compelled to participate in chaos in the first place. They give you something bigger and more sacred to focus on so the rest just falls away.

You can find safety in the Amanita until you find safety within yourself.

If you have OCD behaviors and they are disturbing to you, please see your mental health care provider.

*I've met so many beautiful **colors**!*

CHAPTER 13 *Sun, Water, Earth, & Fire*

This mushroom is the fungi that will ask you to indulge yourself in the things of the earth. The language of this mushroom is sun, water, earth, and fire. There is a reason that many cultures and practices discuss these elements. And indeed, the earth itself uses these elements for healing, shifting the earth itself and its landscape, and for cleansing and healing.

Amanita looks like the sun, has precursors to vitamin D in it, has sun and dark cycles, does photoconversion from ibotenic acid to muscazone in European ones, and does its best work in the soil with mycelium. This is the language it speaks, and when you take Amanita, this is the language it will remind you that you also speak.

> *While you are healing with this medicine, it will be important for you to engage in rituals that involve these elements.*

And indeed, our ancestors, for thousands of years, lived close to these elements as well as using them and fire in rituals regularly. We have become divorced from all of this, and the mushroom's work is to call us all back home to these foundational parts of our humanity.

 ## Sun

Research shows that our exposure to early day sun and early evening sun is important for our mental health and our sleep. The angle of the rays of light at these times of day is what's important. We need to be outside for 10 or 15 minutes exposed to this, and this is a great time for a walk. Using Amanita will also help us with vitamin D, and the additional sun exposure will as well. If there's no illness or reason not to, then be outside in these important exposure times without sunscreen.

Water

The rains bring the fruiting of the fungi, and the water heals us also. Looking at bodies of water can help lower your heart rate and blood pressure and increase feelings of relaxation. Our water today is missing most of the minerals we need, and water is one of our largest sources of minerals we need for mental health. Take time to begin researching your water sources. See if there are natural sources of water near you or even within a few hours' drive. Well water, if the earth is clean, is a valuable source of drinking water.

Look up water sommeliers online, read their work for sources of mineralized water, and educate yourself on water. Make it a point to start some water rituals to get yourself into clean bodies of water. If your water at home is fluoridated and chlorinated, look for natural sources and bodies of water that are clean for you to begin some regular rituals for dunking yourself. This ritual goes back deep into the history of mankind, from cold water dips to rituals for cleansing and letting go to just peaceful floating and time in peace.

Earth

The earth is our original home, and being barefoot on the soil is very important to cleansing, healing, grounding, centering, and moving the work we do. Mycelium of Amanita is a wonderful thing to walk around and on top of. They take the chemical messengers from the surface and use them as information. Creating a relationship with the soil and fungi in your area also leaves messages for the animals who frequent your area.

The more time you spend with your bare feet on the ground, the more you will begin to notice that something important is happening. If you are dysregulated, find some earth and stand on it barefooted. If you can find bare dirt, even better. Grass is better than nothing. While modern society calls this earthing or grounding, I call it being human. Trail walking barefooted is an amazing experience. It's only in the last 50 years that we have started wearing shoes outside every time we go out, even to check the mail or grab something from the car. If you live in a city, there's a good chance your feet haven't touched soil in months or years. The earth's magnetic pull and polarization move in us unless we are creating barriers to it with shoes, concrete, housing, carpets, and socks. Time on the soil can become a really nice ritual to add to your weekly life.

 ## Fire

Fire is one of the most basic and important elements of earth to humans. And we rarely even look at it anymore. If you have ever spent time by a fire, you know its healing capacity. Not only this, but fire is home. Our cultures, societies, tribes, and human ancestors from all over the planet revered fire as the home. Any one tent, structure, cabin, lean-to was not home. The fire was large and central to the community and was the home base for everyone. Family who had been gone, when they returned, the fire became home and where the entire group went to officially cement the return. Food sits over the fire, and drums are played; rituals, dances, alliances, smoking, pacts, trust, hugs, and solace are all here, by the fire.

It is a new development in the history of all of mankind's time on earth to not be by fire every single day. And now we are rarely by fire. Our body knows. If you live in an apartment without a fireplace, it is likely you haven't seen a fire in months or years. Sometimes I wonder, when we have strange cravings that we can't place, and we think it's food, if it is fire. Sometimes when I get these cravings, I will light a candle and see if my body is like, "YES, OMG, please make a fire."

Fire gazing is a practice and a highly valuable experience. When we do equinox and solstice rituals in modern times, we include fire for important, valuable reasons. Many holy modern shamanic places have created ways to have fire because it is so important. Fire gazing can be emotionally difficult. The first hour by the fire can be uncomfortable. But after that, it can bring you into a trance-like state. In that state alone, even without any substances, deep healing happens. You might find that you feel agitated and edgy the next day. This is because healing is happening. Good fire hygiene will help you move the backlog and then maintain good mental health.

All of these contribute to our mental health or our mental illness in its absence. The point of using these fungal friends is that they will teach us where we went off track. They can and will lead you back home, not only by healing what's broken but also by showing you the habits needed in your life to remain healthy. Allow them to teach you how to return home.

WORKSHEET #6: Sun, Water, Earth, Fire

Statement	− ··········· +
I go out in the sun often	
I wear sunscreen all the time	
I go outside in the mornings	
I drink bottled water	
I drink tap water	
I get in water other than to bathe	
I like being outside	
I walk on grass or dirt barefooted	
I sit by fires	
I cook food on a fire	
I have rituals with fire	

Please write the things that you miss about the sun, or water, or fire or the earth.

I know these things may seem like a real pain. Or maybe like they aren't important to your life at all. I mean, you've made it this far, and modern life has created conveniences so these elements really aren't necessary. I hear you. I get it.

> *Using this mushroom is going to change you in many ways.*

One of the ways it changes us is by showing us the true source of our anxiety. It's not always the super obvious things like abuse, lack of sleep, pressure about money, and relationships. If so, we would have easily just worked on those things. And maybe you actually have, and nothing has helped. The wisdom of living medicine that modern medicine cannot understand is that it is a real conversation, a real wisdom holding knowledge from the ancient past of how our human bodies actually work and thrive.

They bring this knowledge, having kept it while we left the forests and earth medicines and daily practices behind from tens of years to hundreds of years ago. We evolved for millions of years as humans with fire, walking on the earth barefooted, being in bodies of water, drinking from bodies of water, and living in the sun. It's only in a few generations that most of us have suddenly departed from all of them. Our bodies don't care about modern convenience. We have no idea how our entire body systems depended on all of these elements separately and as a whole.

The fungi and earth medicines have been holding onto this wisdom and knowledge for us. Some of our original and indigenous cultures still know this and are fully aware of it. But most of us today are completely clueless about how these elements are paramount to our survival and mental health. Allow the mushrooms to remind you of how simple keeping a good balance of mental health can be. Allow Amanita to show you, from within, how using these elements in your ritual will return you to balance.

As you begin to awake inside and start to think to yourself, 'You know, I sure could use a fire,' allow that tiny voice to be the voice of self-love and reason and inner truth. Give it a wide berth. Nurture it like a tiny seedling sprouting. It is YOU. It is your deeper knowing finally surfacing. As you continue your work with Amanita, allow it to continue to inform you. As you listen to the need for these elements, return from deep inside, nurture them, and incorporate them into your life. As I grow Amanita Dreamer, I will continue to incorporate them into my platform, my work, my offerings, my land, and the services I create. How can you incorporate them into not only your personal life but what you offer the world?

Let's brainstorm some places local to you that offer fire. Are there parks, fire ring camping, and yoga studios with outdoor fire? What about even some restaurants with outdoor seating with fireside places? What about wedding venues, coffee shops, or Airbnb? What places local to you offer water rituals or baths? Spas? Float tanks?

Take some time as part of your work in this chapter to get online, ask people you know, and make as long of a list as possible here for your ability and access to the elements of sun, water, earth, and fire. You can also work with others in your area to rent an Airbnb that has a fireplace or firepit that might also be by a water source. You can make a weekend of it. Can you organize a weekend event at an Airbnb where you offer services, like a drum circle and fire ritual? Work with a local massage therapist or healer.

What is available for you to seek out or visit locally? You will need this list so that when you get motivated, it is here, and all you have to do is look at it and grab one as you are building your rituals and gaining strength and motivation. Don't skip this part. Trust me.

#6 Sun, Water, Earth, Fire

Rentals or places to stay or camp for overnights and weekends

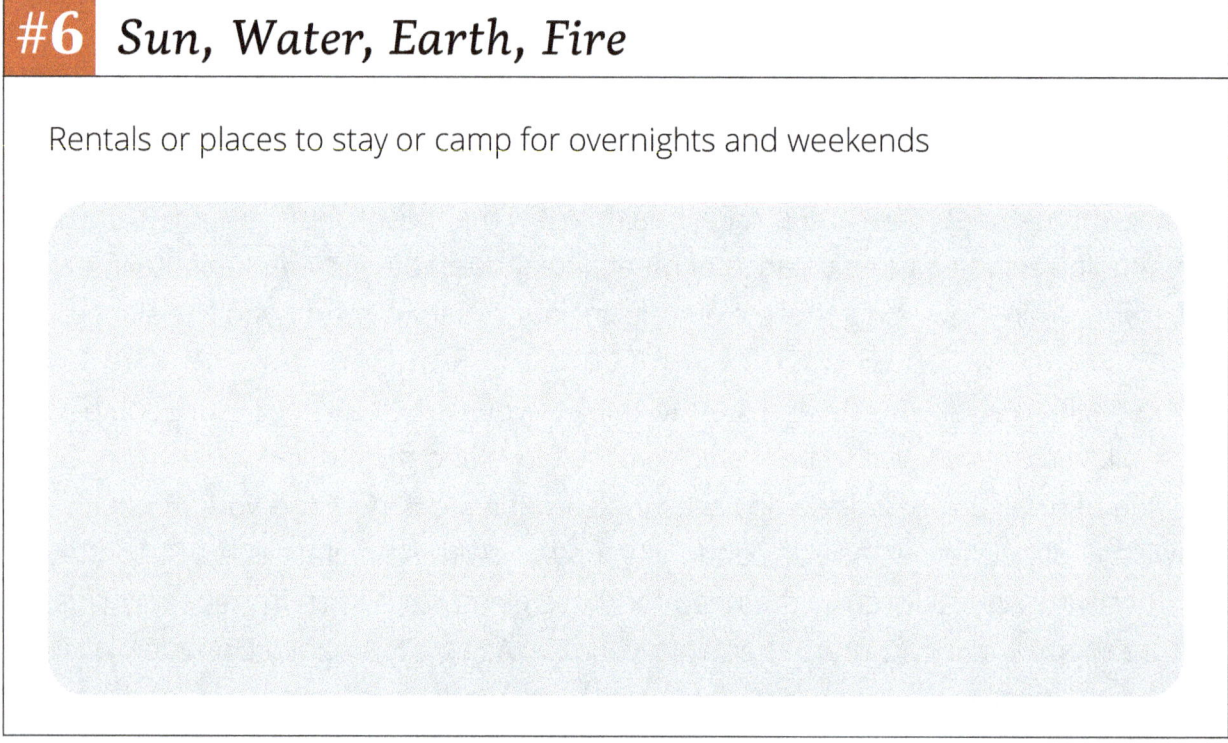

#6 Sun, Water, Earth, Fire

Sun Exposure

Water Bathing

Barefoot Grounding

Fire Gazing

CHAPTER 14

Love & Fear

Amanita is the heart mushroom. The way angst, fear, and anxiety show up in the body is the heart racing, shortness of breath, and tightness in the chest. When we feel love, we can also experience the heart racing, as well as expansion and warmth in the chest. In our bodies, love and fear are opposites, and both are governed by the heart. It's impossible for fear to exist where there is love; for the same reason, it's impossible for a room to remain dark after you've lit a single small candle. We're talking about the energies of fear and love.

> Love is the antidote to fear in the same way that heat is the antidote to cold.

If you're making decisions from a place of fear, you're making decisions from the absence of love. Conversely, when you're operating from a place of love, it's harder to act out of fear. This is what I call "living through your heart," and Amanita will absolutely ask you to live through your heart. Here's an example of how that works.

Think of someone you have (or had) a contentious relationship with. Maybe it was someone who betrayed you, someone who wounded you. What do you feel towards *them*? Anger? Fear? Bitterness? Contempt? Resentment? Unsettled business? Regret? Shame? When you're living through your heart, you'll feel compassion, warmth, kindness, and/or tenderness. You'll feel like extending the benefit of the doubt. It will be easy to believe they're doing the best they can with what they were given and that if they *could* do better, they *would*.

Most of us haven't identified what love feels like in our bodies. We haven't taken time to sit with it and just simply be with it. Mushrooms really grow this part of us and help us begin to learn the difference between infatuation, attraction, and actual love.

Many people think that love means we want to do something with it. We feel drawn to someone, we desire closeness, and we want to make them really happy and help make their dreams come true. We want to make them laugh and solve their problems and be a safe person for their vulnerability and shadow work. While those are *acts* of love, that's not the same as loving them. Most of the time, we're acting out of love for people, but we aren't actually feeling that love because we are preoccupied in our head, or we are feeling fear and anxiety. Or we are rushing (which is emotionally violent, as we've discussed), and our rushing is taking the place of that love.

What Amanita will do naturally for you is create this warmth in your chest randomly for no reason. Sometimes it won't make any sense at all. You'll be busy in the grocery store, and you're in a hurry, and you're thinking about money, and did you even bring the card you need to pay for this? And did you forget anything? And then all of a sudden, someone will walk by and just look at you, make eye contact, and keep walking. And all of a sudden, you see their beauty, and you find yourself thinking things like, 'You know, I think humanity's gonna be okay.' That's living through your heart. Being open to connection with everyone - emotional connection, energetic connection, spiritual connection, you name it. And all it takes is an instant for that connection to happen, and suddenly you're sitting in the truth that we are all connected, not as a concept but living it.

You don't have to do it. Amanita will start doing this for you. So when you come to these rituals, your heart will start to open up naturally, and you'll feel gratitude for the things that are in the cup. You will have more grace for other people or for these difficult times of the day or the difficult day of the week, or just for yourself. This is what it means to live through the heart, to the point where forcing anything feels emotionally violent and allowing feels like love.

Relating to Society while Living Through the Heart

Living this way can be alienating at times, as it's rare that you'll find other people who live like this. There will be people who want you to stay rigid because either it validates their own rigidity, they've come to depend on your compulsions to keep their own life together, or they're just averse to change. They might see this shift as a problem and try to talk you back into your old way of operating. They might abandon you altogether. And if you're living through your heart, you'll let them go.

Others will see your newfound go-with-the-flow-ness as an opportunity to take advantage of you. You're gracious, forgiving, and understanding, so they're going to want to take up every inch of slack you extend them. What these people don't realize is that with Amanita comes self-respect and boundaries. We'll talk about that later in the book.

Mind you, having empathy and fluidity doesn't mean you'll always love the circumstances you're in. But, you will find that you can hold love and empathy while simultaneously not caring for a situation or even feeling angry about it. Set that boundary. Walk away, reset, and start to reevaluate that relationship, and then maybe re-engage when you can do so with compassion and understanding, even if it means you have to part ways. I'm not saying your life is going to be without pain. I'm not saying you won't ever feel afraid. But you will be able to live with integrity, love, compassion, and a gentleness that living in fear prevents.

One thing I've learned from this mushroom is that when it comes to living this human life in these human bodies, pain is necessary, but suffering is optional. Suffering arises from resisting what is. Amanita will help you be present with what is, with openness and acceptance. I know this sounds upside-down, but yes, that even means you'll be open and accepting of the pains that life brings. It's part of being shown what needs work and healing. And what's most important to note here is that you'll be supported by the mushrooms and you will pass through it with more love than you are used to.

As you begin to experience things that feel like living through the heart, write them down here to anchor them, so that you're not letting them pass unnoticed.

So many **shapes** and **sizes**

CHAPTER 15   *Black & White Thinking*

Amanita Muscaria really likes to deal in black and white, yin and yang, and duality. Before encountering this mushroom, I was aware of yin/yang duality. I understood that ancient wisdom was important to several cultures around the world. Still, it never really resonated with me personally as anything other than an idea that made sense for contextualizing things within the principle of opposites.

I find it fitting that this mushroom has two completely opposing medicines (ibotenic acid and muscimol), and they are indeed the two sides of your Fight or Flight System.

> If you just take high amounts of *ibotenic acid*, you're going to get sick.

> If you just take high amounts of *muscimol*, you're going to have an opportunity to do some profoundly deep work that you may not be ready for.

I find it beautiful that the answer lies in the middle. One of the first things you're going to notice is your black-and-white thinking. When you slow down and observe yourself operating from black-and-white thinking and think, 'Oh, I'm being super rigid right now,' you're giving the mushroom permission to do some work. It's going to invite you to live in the in-between. Here's what that looks like.

In Logistics

We spend a lot of time going from place to place. Imagine you're on the road to meet up with a friend, and you've planned to stop at the grocery store first. There's a wreck on the way, and you realize you're going to be late. Black-and-white thinking would tell you that being late is either a good thing or a bad thing (usually bad) as opposed to a neutral thing, which it is. It would then tell you that in order to avoid the bad thing, you need to forego your trip to the grocery store. Living in the gray would say you just need to communicate with the person you're meeting up with and plan your trip around how that conversation goes.

Say you follow black-and-white thinking and forego the grocery store trip. You're putting yourself out either by just going without whatever you need from the store or creating the need to shoehorn a grocery trip into some other plan down the road.

> And that takes a toll on your *nervous system*, your *self-talk*, and your sense of *self-worth*, as well as strengthens any habit you may have had of *putting yourself last*.

Now, say you follow living in the gray in between. Because you called, you discover your friend is also running late and was also planning to go to the store on the way. Because you're going with the flow, you offer to just pick up whatever they need. This takes a load off them because now they can just head straight there and not worry about being late. While you're at the store, since you've slowed down and are being present, you're able to see that one of the items you needed that's normally expensive is marked half off because they're trying to get rid of it. Because you've rescued yourself from the rushing game, you can notice the cashier might be a little stressed, and you can smile at them, thank them, and tell them you hope their shift ends soon.

This is living in the in-between, in the gray middle. You're not assigning good or bad to situations but rather choosing to live comfortably within what things actually are. And when you do this, it causes a ripple effect—you're not stressed about being late, which is transferred to your friend not worrying about being late. Your bank account benefits as well, all because you slowed down and lived in the in-between.

In Conflict

Conflict is a natural part of any relationship. When this happens, and we get triggered, black-and-white thinking wants to position us as the victim and them as the villain.

'They're hurting me. They don't care about my feelings. I'm not feeling heard, and they're not listening. I'm visibly in pain, and they don't seem to care.'

> Do you see how these can be *polarizing*? There's no room for you to have *empathy* for what they're going through.

There is certainly no room for the potential that they aren't actually judging you, nor is anything actually wrong. The trap is that we're often taught that if we do engage with those ideas, we must abandon the notion that our feelings and experiences are also valid. This is black-and-white thinking. You can feel betrayed and scared, and also hold empathy. You can feel victimized, and also safe and grounded.

In Luck

Luck has less to do with what happens to you and more to do with how you perceive it. Most people would consider winning the lottery to be good luck. It might, though, cause anxiety. You might become paranoid that people will only want you for your money. You might get analysis paralysis figuring out how to spend it and end up spending none of it so that your material life is unchanged, but you now carry around more stress. Or, you might end up like most lottery winners, spending all of your winnings on things you don't need and getting so accustomed to seemingly infinite funds that when they finally run out, you've completely lost sight of how to manage money. You end up more broke than you were when you won.

Your attitude toward your circumstances doesn't just influence your luck, and it doesn't just determine your luck - it literally *is* your luck. Say your phone bill comes due, and you've decided bills are bad because they give you stress, because you have anxiety around money, because you grew up in poverty. Black-and-white thinking says you should ignore this bill (which incurs late fees), or maybe it says you should pay it but then stress about how much less money you have (which perpetuates a scarcity mindset that will bleed into areas unrelated to money). Either way, it'll cause stress, which makes small hardships feel like big ones - and make you respond accordingly, often creating even bigger hardships for yourself.

Luck is actually a story you tell yourself. You might look at your life and thinkt you never win anything, bad things always happen, and you can't get ahead. But another person living the same as you might say they are very lucky, pointing to the $5 parking fee that got waived a few days ago or how they've not had to go hungry in a long time and their 15-year-old car is still running. Maybe you have those same experiences, but you're neglecting to count them in luck. The definition of luck is the issue.

It's important to notice what yours is. Is it when things come easy? Is it only applied to games of chance? Do you only apply it when bad things happen so that you stack the deck in favor of your being unlucky? Do you apply luck every time someone helps you, pays it forward to you, and you get green lights, or do you pass those off as insignificant?

Being a victim tends to build on itself, and once established, becomes difficult to change. However, if you are in an abusive situation, this clearly does not apply to you.

> You may not like to hear it, but most people who *feel like victims* of life are the same people who *don't take accountability* for their actions, choices, and things they are actively doing to cause their own suffering and the suffering of those around them. The two tend to go *hand in hand*.

If you get very upset when you are called out or someone tells you you hurt them, are you also a victim feeling like most things are out of your control? The good news is that you can follow this workbook and Amanita, learning to control the things mentioned in this book and stop having to fight to control how people live, the choices they make, how life works out, and whether or not you are lucky. It's a wonderful realization how Amanita can lead us to the causes of our suffering.

Living in the in-between means seeing bills as neither good nor bad but just as exchanges of energy. If you have enough, you pay it and work with what funds you have left over. If you don't, you make a phone call and see what your options are. Maybe you can start today to see that when you pay that bill, you are keeping people employed.

Maybe if there's a problem and you have to call, you can see the person helping you has a family and bills to pay, and they probably have coffee next to them, and they may be tired, but they are helping you the best they can. You might even get excited when that phone bill comes due because you're able to pay it when before you wouldn't have been able to. You'll be reminded that currency is simply a mechanism of energy exchange, and you'll be happy to do your part to keep the energy flowing - to give as you have received. I call money tokens these days. I've been too poor to pay the bills, which means when I could, I felt grateful for water or electricity.

In Trust

Living in the in-between doesn't allow you to let your past define your future. It's here, now, with what is.

People do terrible things every day, and tens of thousands are harmed daily by the choices made by those in power.

Additionally, people do beautiful and healing things every day for each other.

 Neither of these takes away from the other.

Maybe you'll find yourself open to the idea that the customer service rep wants to be excellent at their job so that they can get promoted and better provide for their family, which is a desire you two have in common. Maybe you'll assume the person who picks up the phone got into customer service to actually help people and shift the tides of what it means to be a customer service rep. You have the choice to assume your significant other is hiding their phone because they don't want you to see the gift they're purchasing for you or the surprise party they're planning for you. Maybe you look back at your performance at work, which you know has been above and beyond, and you're open to the possibility that your boss is calling you into a meeting to tell you about the promotion you just earned. Amanita will stretch all of these thoughts for you and ask you to walk into the unknown.

I tell you about these things so that as the new thoughts start to creep in, you won't dismiss them. It's easy to dismiss your newfound trust as wrong, temporary, or unsafe. Now that you know what to expect, my hope is that when these new ideas begin, you will open wide with an appreciation for them and give living in the gray lots of room to blossom. Whether we are changing our circumstances or not, we are changing our thoughts.

It's A Habit, Not A Fix

Do you see how this doesn't serve simplicity and black-and-white thinking? These are higher-order thoughts that are hard to find when you're living in fear. If we've lived our whole lives in Fight or Flight, then in the rare moments we're not in Fight or Flight, we forget to change our thinking to be more complex. It becomes a habit to be rigid and get stuck in black-and-white thinking. Even when we're at rest and feeling safe, it's still habitual to think rigidly. So we have to retrain our thinking. Where the mushroom comes in is it will start to gently prompt you to observe yourself and develop a habit of asking, "Am I in self-preservation mode, or do I feel safe? And which mode of thinking best serves me right now? What's available to me?"

You'll start to notice non-judgmentally when you're in black-and-white thinking. When you catch yourself operating according to your old rigid programming, you might be tempted to beat yourself up or make up a story that you're 'not doing it right,' but that won't be necessary. It's just about noticing your thoughts, behaviors, and patterns and reevaluating them through the lens of 'Is this way of being in my highest good?'

> Amanita is here to nudge you into turning that **question** into a **habit**.

If the answer is no, Amanita is here to help you alter course. The way you arrive in this state isn't through tripping on a heavy dose one time or having a mountaintop experience that changes your worldview. It's about developing a steady, consistent habit of noticing yourself and how you're thinking and non-judgmentally asking if that way of thinking is best for you. And microdosing certainly gives us this. Macrodosing can speed it up; high doses can bring it in faster.

Any of these things being told to us about the nature of reality and working with entheogens will certainly bring it to our attention:

 It's all a game
It doesn't matter as much as I think it does

 It's all karma
It's happening in this life because of what happened in past ones

 It's all orchestrated by a higher power
It's out of my control

 It's a simulation
We're all operating according to our programming

 Everything works out for a reason
What am I really afraid will happen, and why?

Living in the in-between is about releasing your need to know, your need to be right, your need to be certain. Employ these ideas as *possible* counterpoints to the things you think you're certain of, as a tool to dislodge you from those certainties. We're not replacing old ones with new ones. We're getting rid of them altogether. What is the nature of reality? No idea. And I'm okay with that.

Ripple Effects

The beautiful thing is when you can live in the in-between like this, and you refuse to judge yourself for the decisions you've made that weren't in your highest good or the highest good of those around you, you'll find it very difficult to judge others for doing the same thing. And in the same way that you'll have developed the habit of asking if there's a better way, you'll find yourself inviting others into that same line of thinking, free of judgment for how they're currently operating.

You'll catch yourself making up stories about people and, with the help of Amanita, asking yourself, 'Is that story true? Where did it come from?" instead of just instantly believing it. For example, someone's not making eye contact with you. You might be tempted to immediately assume they're too arrogant to look you in the eye. Or maybe they're too scared. The "what" is real, but the "why" is made up. All you know is that they're not making eye contact. You don't know why. It could be that they're neurodivergent and eye contact is so distracting for them that they've learned that the only way they're going to hear what you're saying is if they look somewhere else. Maybe they have auditory processing issues and need to read lips too.

Somebody repeatedly interrupts you. Instead of thinking, 'My god, they're inconsiderate. Do they realize how rude they're being?' you might take a second to ponder that maybe they're having a hard time processing this conversation right now. Maybe their mind is going a mile a minute, and they know if they don't speak a thought as soon as it comes, they'll lose it forever. Maybe instead of getting defensive and putting them in their place, you could start a sidebar conversation about how the two of you can better move through the discussion without so many starts and stops. Maybe they're having a rough day, and their memory is shot today. Maybe kindness and non-judgment, acting as if nothing is wrong or out of the ordinary, will bring you into brand new places in your relationship with others.

When you stop believing all the stories you make up about people (every time you assign a "why" to the things you experience people doing), you create space to be present. You're not defensive because you realize you're not under attack, and you're not motivated to put them in their place because you hold space to believe they're doing the best they can to face the unseen challenges they're up against.

Emotional Complexity

The beauty of living in the in-between is that we let go of the idea that we can only feel one emotion at a time. It's very weird to feel two strong conflicting feelings simultaneously. Adopt a posture of allowing, open your heart, and make room for all of it. Anger doesn't have to displace joy. Grieving a loss while simultaneously having gratitude that you ever had it in the first place is completely natural, even if it's confusing. It's so weird and uncomfortable you'll actually start to notice when people actively fight to shove a new emotion down because they can't hold it in tandem with what they're currently feeling. The healing is in the complexity.

Keep developing this habit, and you'll soon find yourself feeling terrified while hopeful, angry while empathetic, confident while insecure, and stressed while at peace. You'll find that at any given moment, that's a lot to feel all at once. There is a day coming, if you stay the course, where you will sit in the middle of all of that and feel every bit of it equally–not making up stories about the things you feel, not ruminating, not developing secondary emotions (how you feel about the fact that you're feeling what you're feeling)–rather, you'll just simply be with the feelings, and allow them to be with you. The extra gain in this is when you are feeling something negative; your automatic next step will be to ask what other things you are also feeling right now. And it is so cool to find that you also feel other things that feel good. This helps offset the negativity.

You will start to truly understand the beauty in the fact that there is no such thing as objective reality.

If your reality is your thoughts, and your thoughts are radically shifting, then what is reality? If reality is your perception, and your perceptions continue to morph, then what is reality? If reality is what you feel, and you begin to feel completely conflicting things simultaneously, then what is reality?

If you're questioning the nature of reality, you are no longer living in black-and-white thinking. You're no longer living in absolutes, and the more you live in the in-between, the more compassion you're going to have for yourself simply because it'll become impossible for you to hate yourself. The judgments are gone. The made-up stories your inner monologue used to beat you up are gone. You're too busy loving yourself. And you'll know this is true because you'll find it much more difficult to hate other people. You'll see too much of yourself in them.

The Change is Far-Reaching

I'm going to cover networking in greater detail later in this book, but do you see how this leads us toward networking? And that if you don't break free of black-and-white thinking and live in the in-between, you're not going to be an effective networker? This matters because this mushroom is going to ask us to network with each other. That's actually essential for our survival.

I know you may think this is a small thing, but I promise you where you're headed, if you keep working with Amanita, this is going to become everything. You will start to see this in every single area of your life. There won't be any parts of your life that you won't look at and think, 'You know what, that's rigid and black and white. I need to find the in-between."

I promise you that difficulty, angst, and combativeness are in the black-and-white.

I promise you that in the in-between, there is fluidity, there is grace, there is flow, and there is life. This is one of the most valuable gifts Amanita shares with us.

The more that you do this, the more it will build on itself. The lessons will build on each other. The understanding will get deeper. Your inability to tolerate black-and-white thinking will grow to the point where all you will see is the in-between. People who want to throw you back into black-and-white thinking will not find success easily. You will fully see that black-and-white thinking comes from fear and lack. Then, when you start to feel abundant and open, it will be an easy next step to live in the complexities of the in-between. I hope this is where we're headed as humans.

> Amanita is not the answer; Amanita can bring you to the answer.

And you'll find that the answer was inside you all along, so there's no way it can leave you - even after the Amanita does. All of this is in relation to people who are safe.

CHAPTER 16   *Elders & Ancestors*

One of the first things you'll notice, especially when you start smoking the Amanita or taking your macro and even higher doses, is this warmth in your chest and then suddenly feeling like you're not alone, and you will feel this presence around you. It can often feel like many living entities have shown up. People often report feeling like these entities are very ancient and wise. One of the first beings I encountered when I first started smoking it and doing macro and high doses was what I call the *Loki Energy*.

It had a very Nordic feel to it, and it was very childlike in how it joked and laughed. I associate it with the "up" side of the mushroom, the ibotenic acid. Loki has become somewhat of a household name through movies and media. What this mushroom shows me when it comes to Loki is that, contrary to the mischievous, trouble-making, abusive character we've been shown, it's a very loving energy and says, 'Hey, you're supposed to be having fun here.' This energy replaces fear, panic, and anxiety with a desire to play, have fun, tell jokes, dance, celebrate, laugh, hug, and be physically active.

I've noticed as it starts to slow down and I start to get calm, I feel this very deep, heavy, wise, strong energy come through that represents itself as *Thor Energy*. It feels like power. Not the types of things we tend to associate with power like forcefulness, unmovingness, or domineeringness, but power that's grounded in beingness. It's settled and peaceful, knowledgeable, wise, and loving.

Those are the two major entities that show up for me and my lineage is Nordic. This mushroom grows all over the planet. Once you start smoking it and getting into higher and higher doses of the tea, you'll start to feel like you are surrounded by ancient wisdom in amazingly, beautifully large numbers. It can be overwhelming because most of us in the modern Western world have not grown up in a society raising us to be in touch with the elders and the ancestors.

I come from a very staunch science background, so much so that I had eight years of college in the sciences, wrote science textbooks, and taught high school science. Science is what I lived and breathed and did. So the only thing that would make me open up to these ideas, much less put my reputation on the line by publishing them in a book, is a set of powerful experiences so profound that they left me no choice but to believe. And indeed, that's precisely what this mushroom has given me time and time again.

Your experience will be your experience.

You might be totally science-minded and only interested in the chemical interactions this mushroom has with human biology and the neurochemical effects it has as a result. On the other hand, you may be more spiritually minded and excited about the idea of communing with Elders and Ancestors from this and other realms. I hope you feel validated either way but also to open your mind to the possibilities. Remember that this mushroom is the mushroom of opposites and balance. Regardless of which side of that (imaginary) line you're on, staunchly digging in your heels and judging those on the other side betrays the very nature of what this mushroom is here to do in your life. Yes, our experiences with this mushroom can be explained mechanically through our understanding of material science. And yes, our experiences on this mushroom can be explained through spiritual and esoteric philosophy. Neither of these is wrong, but neither of them is whole. It's not either/or; it's both/and. And you're going to need to hold space for that duality for what we're about to dive into.

The Bank

The idea of universal knowledge is not new. Every ancient culture has some version of this in their belief system. They had different frameworks of understanding how it all worked, but there was a time when humans all over the planet were more or less on the same page that there exists some collection of all human learning somewhere, and that we were all contributing to it, and had access to gain wisdom from it.

I used to believe that humans banking ancient wisdom and knowledge was simply a matter of people passing it down generation by generation through the act of teaching our offspring. Things like family recipes or a mom telling her daughter, "This made me sick when I ate it, so you should stay away from it too." Certainly, that social mechanism exists. We are constantly passing down medicinal and culinary knowledge, things that hurt us, and things that help us. And to this day, human cultures do this through storytelling. From ancient mythologies to Aesop's Fables and Mother Goose's nursery rhymes, all the way to Marvel movies, we continue to use storytelling to pass down real truths we glean from our lived experiences on this planet. I used to think that was the only way we passed understanding from one person to the next.

Amanita changed all that.

We humans are working in tandem with the Ancestors and Elders of the mushrooms. As the earth changes, humans change, and problems change. Today we are dealing with very different issues and problems than we were 20,000 years ago, but the solutions remain the same at their core: love, empathy, and compassion. Looking after the most vulnerable among us. Bridging gaps. These are the things the mushrooms bring us back to, time and time again.

There is this continual conversation happening between us and the mycelial entities, in which we are constantly problem-solving, workshopping solutions with them, and then integrating and working it out together. This conversation is all being recorded in the Bank of Universal Knowledge. Because our consciousness itself is our connection to that bank, you're adding to it right now. As you learn from the Amanita and apply those learnings to your specific life situations, you'll be uploading those connect-the- dots epiphanies to Universal Knowledge so that others in similar situations can download that and use it to help them in their lives both while under the influence of the Amanita and after.

In this way, you are also becoming an elder.

If you've ever found yourself working out a problem or trying to find the win/win in a tough situation, and the answer seemed to present itself as a whole, complete thought while you were in the shower or driving on autopilot, that's what this is. You're downloading something someone else uploaded after making it through exactly what you're in the middle of. That's a lot of information to download, but it's also very wise because it is in such large numbers over thousands and thousands of years, so that when you get that knowledge, you know it, and you know it's deep, profound, wise and true, and you feel the love in it. Yes, it is our subconscious, but as the mushroom shows me, it's also the universal consciousness.

The mushroom entities are helping facilitate this by conversing with us on a soul level and getting us through our tough spots. The more people reconnect with this long-forgotten bond we once had with them, the faster this will happen. This is the wisdom of the gods, the ancestors, and the elders. It is so much more than your genetic ancestors who spoke words to you. It is an ancient, universal experience that you are adding to. When you're gone, you become part of those elders and ancestors that show up for the humans in the future who use it. The trauma we're bringing onboard and the healing we're doing in response will echo forward so that even if you have no biological lineage, you will someday be an Ancestor who has helped all of humanity just by working out your own life.

> There will always be a voice asking if it's just our brains making these experiences up, and asking if any of it is "real."

When you hear that voice raise those questions, consider why it might be that millions of people across thousands of years have experienced (and are experiencing) these exact same things–the same voices telling them the same stories. It lines up quite nicely with the exact same thing that indigenous cultures all around the globe across countless generations have experienced over the years.

If it has created peace, calmness, and mental health, then perhaps that's how we're made. If the experiences I've had because of entheogens are all in my head, that doesn't take away from the fact that that's the story that's keeping me mentally healthy. And that perhaps mental health is more than having a good upbringing or taking the right pill.

Drums

One of the most surprising things the Amanita did was show me how important drumming and ceremonies are. I don't mean ceremony as in alone in the darkness. I mean ceremony, as in lots of people with fire, dancing, and drums in an ancient ritual with the solstices and equinoxes. The first instrument we ever heard was the heartbeat of our birth mother. Drums are some of the first instruments ever made. We have evolved as humans on earth for millions of years, having drums, playing drums, hearing drums, and using them in dance, celebration, ritual, and healing. I followed the mushroom voice, the instruction, and the humans who knew and trusted the process.

And indeed, we can heal with just Amanita. We can have fun and a catharsis with a good beating on a drum. We can heal together singing around a fire. But something very powerful and important happens with all of them together. Something new and different is created when humans come together with drums around a fire. And if it is on a solstice or equinox, the power in it is hard to describe.

Smoking Amanita, with this, creates a piece of the puzzle that brings in elders and ancestors in a more ceremonial way where trance-like states emerge, with the fire entity, the elders swirling about, the visions of our fellow humans around us, blurry and fading in and out as we beat our drum rhythmically, trancing inside, swaying, moving. The unearthing, ascending, flushing, healing, and opening that happens is nothing short of miraculous. This is one of the very first things the Amanita asked of me: "Go tell the people about this. We miss you, and we miss this, and we want you back."

They showed me how important it is for our health and our communities. It is also important to drum alone. Smoking Amanita and drumming is an important ritual we can do with our animals, family, a few friends, or alone. Along with the tea or cacao, or stacking with other herbs like blue lotus, using incense and music, do what you feel led to do as long as you have drums. I have created a drumming playlist linked to Spotify on my website so you can listen to different cultures of drumming and styles to play along with if you need it.

I hope you get involved in drum circles in your area and maybe start one. I hope you find a drum that is important; handmade, and ceremonial for you. I hope you allow the drums to become part of your ritualistic practices.

High dosing is a very important part of the gifts of the Amanita. I understand it can be scary, but consider it graduation when you feel like you can walk through that door.

Maybe fearful, maybe curiouser and curiouser.

And if so, I will see you down the rabbit hole!

CHAPTER 17

Networking

One of the more surprising things the mushroom showed me was how interconnected we are. As an autistic person and coming from a place of isolating myself into suicidal ideation and planning, I wasn't too happy to hear that I would need others to heal. Five years later and I still struggle with this, but today I network like a beast, and I travel and have friends around the globe. I understand now, when what I am missing isn't a food or snack or adventure but people and interaction. We are a social animal which means our mental health and wellness is tied to our connections to others.

Giving

One of the things that the Amanita is going to show you is how important transacting, giving, and receiving is for humans. The problem is that many people view giving as an avenue for deception or manipulation. Some view it as solely transactional: "I give to get." This can cause us to withdraw completely from being willing to receive and feeling weird about giving. And for sure, we all need to learn discernment.

Transactionalism

How many times in your life have you been cleaning the house, which led to organizing, which led to downsizing, and all of a sudden you have all this stuff you want to get rid of, so you start giving it away to friends and family, maybe even strangers. How do people react? I'm sure most people would instantly refuse, either because they don't want to put you out like that or they don't have anything to give in return–they would feel guilty just taking this thing that you've explicitly stated you'd like to give them for free. People who react that way see your relationship (and maybe all their relationships) as transactional. They don't want to take it because they'll feel like they owe you, and they don't want some imaginary debt hanging over them, especially when they have no intention to even the score.

Maybe you operate that same way because you, too, have been brought up to believe relationships are transactional by nature. Maybe you do favors for people and secretly count on them to return said favors when you hit a tough spot. Or maybe you've been conditioned by a wounded caregiver to be attentive to the needs of others but not even know what you need, much less ask for it.

These transactional attitudes are very rigid and black-and-white. Even if you're just a naturally generous person known for being selfless, there's likely a part of you that has a deep-seated need to identify as a charitable person, and every time you give of your time, money, energy, or possessions, that need is fed, and the identity is locked a little more into place. You certainly stand to gain a *lot* from all that giving.

Non-transactionalism

A flowing, non-transactional behavior would be something like this: say you have a high-value item–something you paid a lot for. You don't want it in your life anymore, and you don't have time to sell it. Most people hold on to it, waiting to find time to sell it, and it winds up taking up space. A new attitude you will find with Amanita is the idea that you can just give away a high-priced item. You hold onto it, and you find someone you know would love it, and you just give it away. You don't ever mention it again, and you don't ask them how they like it; you want nothing in return–not even the satisfaction of knowing they appreciate the gift. You simply wanted them to have it; you created a reality in which they have it, so the mission is accomplished, and the case is closed. You don't ruminate on it after the fact, wondering if you should've sold it or how much you could've made on it. Regrets don't creep in. You won't start wishing you still had it or feel like you wasted the gift on the person you gave it to.

The mushroom mycelium moves precious nutrients around for themselves, for the trees, and for all living things. While they transact, when they work with baby trees, they do much more giving than they receive.

Non-transactional love is saying "I love you" and meaning it without feeling the need to hear it back or feeling insecure or disappointed if you don't. It means doing something kind for someone without expectation of gratitude, reciprocity, or even acknowledgment. It's the donor who gives anonymously. It's the friend who drops a bottle of wine off at the door of a friend when they hear they've had a rough day. It's taking care of someone's needs simply because you want their needs met, not because you hope they'll meet yours in return.

When we start out by giving of the things we don't need and of the things given generously to us, we learn first how to get out of transactional thinking. We learn the joy of moving precious resources around to help others. It's wonderful to have, say, a nice jewelry box made of wood, ready to give to thrift when someone at a meet-up randomly says they are in need of one. When you can say, "You'll never guess what I have in the car to take to donate. You're welcome to it," and they love it, you will learn how amazing it feels to be part of the manifesting for another person. The more you do this, the more rapidly it will happen that your goods find their new owners.

Giving freely is so important to survival for us. So much so that if you don't allow other people to give to you, you are taking away their human right to give and to feel good about giving, and creating cohesiveness, trust, and safety as a human. This is what creates those things for us as humans. Crows give gifts, dogs give gifts, birds give gifts, cats give gifts, and babies give gifts. It is written into the social animals' survival as a necessity.

When you become fully integrated with the craft of giving freely, it means you'll be able to receive freely without feeling indebted, guilty, or unworthy. When people, or just the universe, share gifts with you for free, you'll be able to feel the magic of what it's like to be on the receiving end. You can say "yes" with openness, without looking for what strings are attached.

Giving is such a basic human need, we even have a reward for it baked into our brain chemistry.

They call it the "helper's high," and you literally flush with endorphins when you believe you've done something genuinely altruistic for another living thing. When you learn to give like this, you'll also realize that the very act of rejecting gifts (whether the gifts are objects, time spent, or energy spent) robs people of their innate need to give. And as a giving person yourself, you'd never in a million years dream of depriving someone of the joy that comes with that. You'll start to see how a community of freely giving people creates a network of trust and gratitude, which is a net strong enough to catch anyone who might otherwise fall through society's cracks.

Once you learn what this way of giving and receiving feels like, you will learn how to recognize the energy and signs of someone attempting to give transactionally with manipulation in mind. You will learn boundaries to say "no, thank you. I don't need it." If you miss it and wind up on the end of them asking for favors you can't provide, you will also find the courage and strength to say "no" and allow them to think poorly of you.

Reciprocity

The other way of giving is reciprocity. In this exchange, there is much raising of energy and love. Let's say Marco is a shaman of psilocybin, and he wants to do more work in the community and make a name for himself, coming out into the world to provide this service to his community. And let's say you have a bunch of heirloom seeds you inherited from your grandparents. When you meet Marco at a yoga class, he tells you about his new endeavors. You tell him you have been needing to journey but haven't found the right place or time. He mentions to you how he just started a garden, and he really wants to grow heirloom foods. You can offer your seeds, and he can offer his services for a journey.

> Trades like this are in the highest good for all, will start becoming effortless, and will start happening more often as we begin to heal and use our earth medicines.

It will become unbelievable how often we find these perfect matches that make dreams come true and facilitate everyone being happier. As a cherry on top, they usually wind up being actions that bring in other people too, fulfilling *their* dreams, and creating more spaces for even more people to get involved in it. Seeds planted in the meeting of two people coming together in reciprocity tend to grow gardens of food and opportunity for the community to find what they needed too. Not-for-profit foundations get formed, banks of resources for communities, drum circles that turn into classes that turn into an educational foundation become how we build the new world. You never know how a single chance exchange of reciprocity can turn into an amazingly good friend with whom you share and grow a business or networking, connecting others, growing their reach in their dreams, and building what they feel is their role in society while they just keep sending amazing people and opportunities your way too.

Reciprocity is of the highest good and is the ultimate in the exchange we will learn to trust and be a grand part of moving forward in our healing. We get there by first learning to let go of the things that no longer serve us freely, without wanting anything in return. We grow by allowing others to give to us in the same way. We graduate to reciprocity, leaving transactional giving far behind. We become like the mycelium, networking for the higher good of all.

Networking

The Amanita Muscaria mushroom is The Great Networker. It works with the trees to get nutrients from the soil to feed the trees and get sugars that the tree makes as a trade. It also sends signals, information, and nutrients through its mycelium to baby trees from elder trees. It sends signals from tree to tree. It works with bacteria in the soil that it needs to grow. It works with humans to help us heal, and it accepts our transport of spores to help it travel from its origins in Siberia to eventually cover the globe. It teaches us to network, to learn, to introduce people to each other, to reach out and help to pass things on, and to share in the same way they do. They tell us it's vital to our survival and that we have forgotten this about our past, and they wish for us to remember.

> If you use Amanita, you may find that you want to start networking.

Be prepared to feel urges to give freely of your time. Be prepared to remember what people tell you and to connect these random things. Be prepared to collect items and relationships and find yourself being on the lookout for who needs what. Do they need something you've picked up along the way and have been carrying around in your car for months? Do they need to be connected to someone you know?

This is what I mean when I talk about networking. I'm not necessarily referring to the kind of networking you hear about in the corporate world where you attend mixers and swap business cards with strangers with whom you have entire conversations consisting of rehearsed elevator pitches and forced laughs at bad jokes. There's nothing wrong with those per se, but the networking I'm talking about is more along the lines of loving people, being interested in people, seeing their value and the value they could add to the world, and being like a switchboard operator from the pre-phone number days, hooking people up to other people and forming connections that set everyone up to get where they're trying to go.

It's you saying to the Universe, "I am open. Use me however you'd like. I am here to be the connection." You are there to be the network. The mushrooms say you are just like the mycelium. While you are an individual sentient living thing, as a human network, you are a consciousness–a larger living thing, and you connect with others in more than just the spoken word.

We're all tapped into the same consciousness. We're all branches on the same tree.

So when your neighbor down the street suddenly realizes her grandmother has passed away right about the same time you get the urge to make oatmeal cookies, don't be surprised when later that week, you're at the coffee shop snacking on your homemade oatmeal cookies, and your neighbor walks in and starts crying, and then tells you that her grandmother used to make oatmeal cookies all the time and she was just thinking that morning how much she'd love some just so she can have that feeling again. And, of course, you made more than you can eat, so you tell her you'll bring her some later that day.

I'm not saying we don't have free will or that our every move is orchestrated by some higher power pulling the strings. Picture it like the roads. There are road signs and stop lights, and lines painted on the concrete that all mean specific things to keep the traffic flowing. And everyone on the road has the choice at all times whether to turn left or right, enter and leave the roads and when to go back home. And when everyone goes with the program, the traffic flows freely. Humanity is a complex system that can run like a well-oiled machine when we surrender to the flow and live how our Elders and Ancestors advise us. And when you do follow their guidance and live through the heart, all these synchronicities will start to happen. You'll go from feeling like you're swimming down a river to feeling gently but briskly pulled by its current, simply able to relax and enjoy the ride.

It's all energy. And when this mushroom asks you to network, you're going to see that it is very much not in a strong-arming, forcing-it-to-happen kind of way but in a more energetic, flowing way. You will find that the things that work are so much more profound and for the higher good of all that so much of your experience and existence becomes reciprocity, and it becomes flowing and beautiful. You're going to meet the most beautiful people, and in doing so, you're going to bank all of these amazing connections. You are becoming an elder. Every moment you've lived prior to today, you have already become an elder to others who will experience what you've already experienced, but also to yourself.

At the end of the day, you'll start to network because your physical actions in tangible space and time will start to reflect the inner transformation the mushroom will be inviting you to make. And as you integrate further and further into the Oneness that is all of life, you'll start to realize in a new, embodied way how connected we all are. And if you're living authentically through the heart when you have those realizations, becoming a master networker is the next logical step you'll take. You'll go from creating connections to being Connection itself. And the Mushroom Voice loves to help get you there.

> It's all about connection.

Ancestors

CHAPTER 18 — Time - Part 2

One of the things that you'll see early on in using Amanita is these blips of time. Time jumps. And when you microdose, you may, for a moment, just for a moment, see things the way they are in the very, very near future, like a couple of seconds from now or the recent past, like just a couple of seconds ago. Or if you're going downstairs, all of a sudden, you may almost fall because you're suddenly at the bottom of the stairs, and then suddenly you're back three steps up from where you just were. It may just be like a blip. And these things happen pretty early on. Time will briefly distort, just enough to make you wonder how much time has just passed.

Other times, it will seem time is speeding up or slowing down. It may be small fluctuations in seconds and minutes, or it might be large fluctuations where you go from Monday to the following Wednesday and back again in what feels like a handful of minutes. This usually happens early on when you start taking Amanita, and I need you to know that this is normal.

You may read this and think, 'I don't want to live like that. It would only add to my anxiety!' What Amanita wants to do is show you what is anchoring you to your anxiety. And in large part, for most of us, the biggest culprit is our attachment to this concrete idea of the passage of time. Amanita is trying to teach you a whole new way of seeing the world and a whole different way of being in it. One of the things they hope you'll learn from this experience is that time is not a measure of distinct temporal proportions that are equal outside of you, but rather, time is you.

> *You are the creator of realities, and you are time.*
> *Therefore, time does not exist outside of you.*

Just as your brain creates the experience of sound to make sense of the external stimuli caught by your eardrums, time is something your consciousness creates to make sense of your interactions with the physical world. Thus, everybody's internal clock is as unique as their fingerprint. The way your brain creates time to organize its

> In the same way, time is a way of experiencing reality, not an intrinsic property of reality.

experience will fluctuate as you move throughout the day. This is always happening. But because we've created government time and perpetually force each other to get in sync with it, we're completely blind to these fluctuations in the same way your brain is blind to most of the information your eyes take in through your peripheral vision.

One example of this is if you listen to podcasts or audiobooks at 2x speed. People who consume content will double the speed they listen because it matches their internal rhythm and how they perceive it. Others like to slow it down to take in every nuance and let each word hang. Noticing that we each move at different speeds internally as well as physically is the first step toward realizing how much more there is to time.

Some mornings you might spring out of bed and get a whole day's worth of productivity accomplished in the first three hours of being awake. You'll sit down, look at the clock, and gasp at the fact that it's still morning. Other times you'll wake up, look at the clock and see that it's 7:00, rub your eyes, stretch, go to the bathroom, and look at the clock only to see that it's now 8:30. This isn't just you being super energetic in the first example and super lethargic in the second. You literally created time at a faster or slower pace for yourself relative to government time.

Everybody is different in the way they create time, how they move, how they talk, how they process things, the speed at which they actually move their bodies, the speed they want to drive, and the speed they want to walk. Naturally, these differences exist because we all have different time inside our bodies. There are no other animals that keep time the way humans do. Yes, most pack animals tend to move at the same pace and the same speed as each other. There's very little variation and difference. Yet humans are the only animals that can hold a rhythm and maintain a beat to partial seconds accurately. Some species of birds get close, but we are timekeepers in a very unique way to this planet. Most animals don't think about time. Creatures in the animal kingdom flow, they live, they move, they eat, they walk, they crawl, they dig, they burrow, they fly, and they swim. Animals eat and move and hide and hibernate. They're flowing with an overall rhythm of the earth's 24-hour cycle.

Humans invented the idea of time so that we could coordinate. "Meet me in X location, Y days from now." We want to come together for celebrations, and we plan them regularly. We use the solar system around us to help mark when these events are, and we have developed elaborate timekeeping pieces to do this. We have slowly crept up on our distancing from natural time. Early on, we could say, "Meet me at this rock in 3 days when the sun sets." Later sundials could make it easier to say when during the day to meet, given a range of about an hour. Clocks and watches made it possible to begin to time trains within a 15-minute window, and eventually, with satellites, we have time clocked down to seconds.

> We love time. We are time. We play in the space-time continuum. That's why we're here - to play in it.

When we are forced to exist in an arbitrary model of time where we all have to set an alarm, get up and make our brains work, go out and get in large metal vehicles and sling ourselves across town at high speeds trying not to get injured, only to show up somewhere and participate in a system in which our ability to have food and shelter depends on our ability to march to the beat of someone else's drum, do you see how this could lead our bodies to revolt against us? No wonder so many of us have anxiety and burnout!

The Amanita says, "You'll be most productive doing tasks that are best for you when you do so with the timing that matches who you are. As a result, you'll be living the life you were meant to live, and you'll live it to its fullest." As humans, our bodies naturally want to move with the sun and with our natural rhythms. The things you'll learn in this chapter may be a little uncomfortable to integrate because it may make you weird, and people may deem you unfit for corporate life or modern society. The good news is, more and more people are doing that every day, to the point where the ever-growing cultural narrative is that it's actually our society that's broken for not accommodating all the different ways people operate instead of people being broken for not fitting into the way society operates.

From this perspective, outside of time, you'll see how much of your anxiety came from the time others imposed on you. You'll see your depression, your lethargy, your

Not to worry, though. You won't stay here. This isn't your new normal.

chaos, your scatteredness, your stress, your panic, your worry, and you'll see just how much of it was tied to your constant scramble to keep up with someone else's timescale while abandoning and rejecting your own.

The reality is you still exist in a human body on a planet that takes 24 hours to rotate on its axis and 365¼ days to orbit around the nearest star. And you're still in a system where trading your hours for dollars is the thing that puts food on the table for many people. So once you've been knocked out far enough to turn around and see it for what it really is, you'll be able to return and re-integrate, but now you'll be fully aware of your true inner pace with the need to protect it with boundaries. You will learn when to set them, when to live in an external time, and how to navigate it

The goal is to find yourself being aware of where you are in government time but not feeling the need to chase it around or snap your life into its rigid containers. Hopefully, you won't set out to be productive; you'll set out to flow. And you'll find that in that flow, you'll actually be more productive than you were before and less stressed about it. It won't be "What time do I need to go to sleep in order to wake up in time to get to work on time." Instead, it'll be, "I can feel my body starting to wind down. I'm gonna follow its lead so that I can get a super restful sleep tonight."

Time Manipulation

One thing that is going to be integral to your freedom and safety is your ability to manipulate time. Remember that time is something your consciousness creates to make order of your experiences. Time itself is an experience you create for yourself. And as we've covered already in this chapter, you already experience yourself speeding up and slowing down your time relative to government time.

Einstein spoke of relativity in terms of time seeming to pass very slowly when your hand is on a hot burner and time passing very quickly when you're spending time with your lover. His explanations of how time passes differently in different gravity are really cool. There are things that expand and contract our experience of time, and we've even accepted that as a society, more or less. What I'm saying is that once you realize this is actually what's happening, you can learn to control how slowly or quickly you create time for yourself.

Step 1: Stop Resisting

The first thing you'll need to do is develop a habit of noticing when you're in resistance to what is. You're not wrong for being in resistance. These are your core values, and you're not wrong for having those. What I'm saying is you won't be able to manipulate time while you are in resistance to what is.

> It's about learning to notice when you're in resistance and then asking yourself if resistance is your best choice for this moment.

You're resisting because someone hurt you or you feel threatened. You get into resistance when you fear you'll lose something you want to keep, even though your possession of it has always been an illusion. Stress, anxiety, "shoulds", and rushing are good indicators that you might be in resistance. So notice when you're in resistance and ask yourself why. Your ability to do this work is a fundamental requirement of time manipulation.

Step 2: Lean In

Once you've got that down, the next step is to learn how to lean into what's happening. Whereas resistance is an active movement away from what's happening, you're going to replace that compulsion with the decision to actively move into what's happening. If you don't do this with intention, then even if you're not resistant, you may still be indifferent. You can't manipulate time from a place of neutrality either. You have to be in it. I'm not saying it's going to be all sunshine and roses. You'll get to choose whether or not to lean into feelings that trigger you. Lean in, and feel everything there is to be felt in this moment, even if it all sucks. All we're doing is learning how to lean in versus resist. That's it. Play with resistance, play with leaning in, and note the differences in what each one feels like.

When you encounter a feeling you'd normally resist, practice this like a new skill you're just starting to learn. Do it in small doses, and then do it more and more as your nervous system allows.

Step 3: Allow

Remember, you have Amanita now. You're not just white-knuckling your way through life anymore. Now that you're on Amanita, when you get that trigger and want to resist, simply say to the Amanita inside you, "Please help me feel grounded and centered." You're not looking to change or escape your circumstances or what's happening to you. You're simply looking for help in adopting a posture of surrender. They want to teach you to reclaim the sovereignty over your own experience that you've always had and use that sovereignty to choose to lean in and allow the moment to be what it is, with peace and flow.

> Entheogens are powerful allies, and they work with you. This is a whole new way of living.

Remember how I said living in pain all the time is absolutely not part of the process? Remember when I told you Amanita doesn't want you to suffer? Remember when I said Amanita is the heart mushroom? Remember when I said it is the self, the ego, the groundedness mushroom, the boundary mushroom? It's not doing that to you. It supports your divine right to do it for yourself by claiming ownership. Suffering is absolutely not a necessary part. Lean in, allow, and give it room.

Pain is inevitable. Suffering is optional.

Once you can take the chaos and just will it to go, you'll start to understand how you and Amanita are working together. This will be the beginning of you manipulating time. Everything we've done in this chapter so far has just been clearing the plate. Taking out the trash. Getting your mind out of the way so that you can actually do what I'm going to show you.

Step 4: Wield Your Sovereignty

This won't make sense until you've done entheogens, but you're not going to manipulate the passage of time for anyone but yourself. You're not going to think of it like something you're manipulating so much as something you're wielding.

Now that you've gotten to a point where you're not habitually standing in resistance to what is, and you've learned to lean in and allow, there will still be moments that you'll want to stretch and experience for longer or moments you want to squish and get through sooner.

A long plane ride, an annual training at work, waiting for a package to arrive that you're really excited about. What you're going to do to get through these faster is to simply think in your mind, "I'd like to get through this part faster." That's it. You just see yourself arriving at the end of the situation right now. You'll start to have sketchy memories. All of a sudden, you'll be standing somewhere and wondering how you got there. What happened was you got through the past 20 minutes in the blink of an eye. Maybe the last hour. Maybe the last day. You can still access your memories from that period, like recalling a dream right after you woke up. It's not like you just went catatonic and stopped making memories, so it would appear that you skipped time. Your consciousness just sprinted through it because you willed it to be so.

Likewise, if it's something amazing and beautiful that you really want to keep holding on to, to experience, you can slow time down and really soak it in. Playing on the floor with your toddler when it suddenly hits you that someday they'll be grown and move out. Seeing your favorite artist in concert. Having an all-night heart-to-heart with a trusted old friend. That last hug before you depart from your loved one at the airport. That first hug when you're reunited again. As soon as you open your arms, think to yourself, 'I want to soak in this moment. I want to feel it in slow motion.' You'll go in for the hug and catch the scent of their hair, and you'll re-live memories from your past together as you feel their heartbeat sync up with yours. You'll feel the love that's moving between the two of you with profound gratitude. You'll feel the two of you get bigger and grow and expand, and you'll feel the past, this moment, and the future all blending into one. You'll feel it go into the ground, and you'll feel the energy of the two of you grow, and then all of a sudden, you'll find yourself wondering how long you've been holding each other because by now, it feels like an eternity.

It's Not Escapism

One thing I hear quite often is that what I'm describing sounds a lot like escapism and refusing to feel your emotions. Suffering is not supposed to be a part of this process. And I'm not saying you're not growing and learning. I'm saying, can you not still allow the Amanita to do the work that it needs to do in really fast time so that you do not have to feel it in long, slow motion? Leaning in and feeling is a necessary part of the process. You're still in it, and you're not escaping anything. You're not avoiding it by going around it or running in the other direction. You're still going through it; but maybe you'd like to get through it sooner than later.

Could you not say, "'I want my bones to heal faster," and speed through to the part where they're healed? Taking pain meds to dull the pain of an injury isn't sitting in rejection of what is; it's simply doing what's in your control to improve your experience of the situation. These are the edge of what seems like reality and what we have control over.

If we can do this with our feelings, can we do it with our bodies?

I know. It gets weirder.

Let's take this time manipulation thing even further. If you can manipulate time inside yourself, if you can decide you want to slow time down and feel this completely, or speed time up and move through something, can you not visit yourself yesterday or tomorrow? If you are time, can you not move yourself inside yourself to another time? Because I can tell you when you macrodose or take heroic doses of Amanita, what you're going to do at some point is fracture and see multiple times of your life, multiple views, experiencing multiple realities simultaneously.

When this happens, it's not just you manipulating time. It's a hundred of you moving forward and backward, watching things unfold, choosing different outcomes, watching them happen, troubleshooting, workshopping, and observing the results of trial and error. And the minute you think about what's happening and realize what's going on, it will all collapse back into just this one you, living in just this one time, the same way that electrons can bilocate until we actually look at them and they collapse back in on themselves. It's the noticing of consciousness that creates it in a moment in time. At this point, words will begin to fail to adequately describe that, and it will become something you will need to experiment with upon the use of higher doses.

As you learn to navigate this space and relax into the reality that there are countless yous working in countless places on countless timelines, you have the fantastic opportunity to pick one and step into it. If you can pick one over here in this second or over there in that second, how about picking one over here 10 seconds ago?

If you are doing this all the time and are just not aware of it, what if you could choose to be aware of it?

If you can pick 10 seconds ago, pick a day ago. Just make sure you stay with what's happening because the moment you start to freak out about the fact that you can go anywhere in time, you'll jump back out of it.

Once you learn to wield time at this level, you can lose your temper in the morning because you didn't get good sleep, and then that afternoon go back to this morning and coach yourself into self-soothing, or even go further back to last night and urge yourself to get to bed earlier so that you'll wake up more rested.

This gets easier once you've truly begun to live through your heart on a regular basis. Live through your heart, be present in what is, and meet life with openness, love, and acceptance. Of course, trying to do this if you're full of fear is difficult, which is why one of the first things Amanita wants to do is get rid of the fear, anxiety, and resistance and teach you to lean in.

This Is Our Birthright

These were yours all along. Our ancestors lived like this. This is how they got wisdom. You have no idea the wisdom that you have, that you can give yourself information, that you can ask yourself about things. This is some advanced stuff, but there's nothing saying that you can't do it. So as you get more familiar with Amanita and the mushroom voice, keep experimenting, keep trying all of the different ways that you can take it and work with it and have relationships with it, and every time you get a new blip, pay attention. Listen when you feel the flow. Allow it to inform you and learn to recognize it as the portal.

Think of how your life will be when you have full access to these tools and have experience in using them. You're in love, living from the heart, in flow, having reclaimed your own sovereignty over your own life and timescale, you're having conversations with the Elders and the Ancestors, and you're moving back and forth through time to talk to past and future versions of yourself, and doing this all with a sense of ease, lightness, and freedom from all the things that bogged you down when you cracked open this book for the first time.

Imagine that.

The *beauty* of these mushrooms!

CHAPTER 19 — *Power & Ego*

We've talked before about Amanita being the power mushroom in Mario. There's a reason that's the powerup symbol. It really is the power mushroom.

> *That includes your power and your divinity, but also your anger and your rage.*

Amanita brings back ownership of your right to be in your body and take up space, to set boundaries and keep them, and to create what the world needs you to create by owning your divinity, body, and rights through the ego. These all seem like separate topics, but they are actually all the very same topic.

Consider the following questions:

- Do you struggle to ask for what you want?
- Are you able to set a fair price for the things that you give or that you make?
- Is it difficult for you to say "no"?
- Do you take action when the time is right?
- What does power look like to you? Is it corrupt? Arrogant? Beautiful? Evil? Necessary?
- Do you feel that power and darkness are one and the same?
- Do you fear powerful people?
- Are you a powerful person?

If you use Amanita long enough, the mushroom will ask you these questions. And these questions are more complex and layered than they seem at first because there are different kinds of power. Please take a moment to rate the following measures of ego and power.

Worksheet #7: Power

Place a mark corresponding to how strongly you feel each statement.

Statement	− to +
I can't get ahead in life	⊖ · · · · · · · · · ⊕
Things always happen to take my money	⊖ · · · · · · · · · ⊕
The universe hates me	⊖ · · · · · · · · · ⊕
I catch all the red lights	⊖ · · · · · · · · · ⊕
People betray me a lot	⊖ · · · · · · · · · ⊕
Everyone takes me for granted	⊖ · · · · · · · · · ⊕
I can't make friends	⊖ · · · · · · · · · ⊕
My time off always gets ruined	⊖ · · · · · · · · · ⊕
If it can go wrong, it will	⊖ · · · · · · · · · ⊕
No one helps me	⊖ · · · · · · · · · ⊕
Rich people were born lucky	⊖ · · · · · · · · · ⊕
The government is keeping me down	⊖ · · · · · · · · · ⊕
Every day is a bad hair day	⊖ · · · · · · · · · ⊕
I look old	⊖ · · · · · · · · · ⊕
Life is just working until you die	⊖ · · · · · · · · · ⊕
I hate my job	⊖ · · · · · · · · · ⊕
No one understands me or listens	⊖ · · · · · · · · · ⊕
I can't even find how to start to change	⊖ · · · · · · · · · ⊕
Every new thing I try fails	⊖ · · · · · · · · · ⊕
I really just wish I could die now	⊖ · · · · · · · · · ⊕

#7 Power

What do you need right now to feel like you have some control over your life?

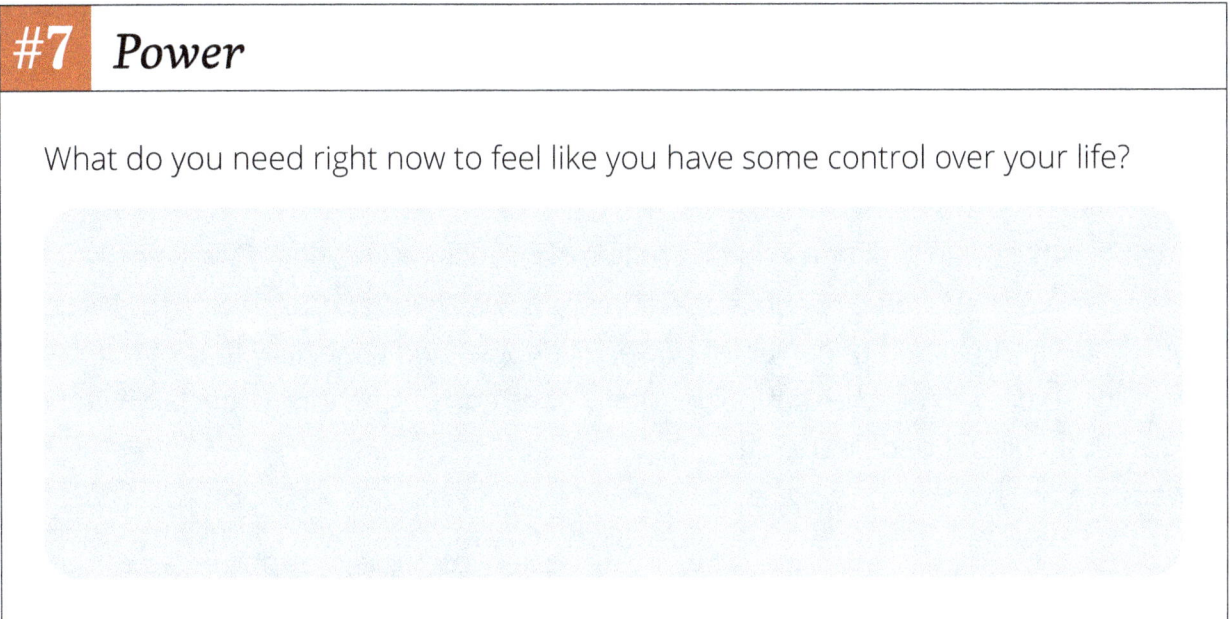

Power Over

When discussing power over, think of someone with the power to arrest you or the power to fire you, the power to take away your ability to put a roof over your head and eat. This is the type of power some parents exert over their kids or bosses over their employees. It's an authoritative power in which they steal (or are given by someone who stole) part of what was supposed to be your sovereignty. You answer to them, you depend on them, and they have the power to drastically affect your life circumstance, where you do not have the same power to do so for them. At some points in your life, you will have power over others. Having this power doesn't mean it is automatically bad. Abusers will use this to abuse; it's low-hanging fruit. But positions of power over can also be beautiful experiences.

Power To

Then there are people who wield an incredible amount of energy and don't seem to participate in things like having obstacles or thinking things are impossible. These are people who seem capable of doing inhuman things, whether operating on very little sleep, lifting more weight than their body size would indicate, or being highly persuasive and influential from their sheer charisma. They're the type of people who walk into a room and command attention without having to do anything but exist–and they grab people's attention because you can feel their presence before they even enter the room. Think of a power outlet in a house. It's quiet, unassuming, and out of the way but capable of supplying energy to everything in the house that needs electricity. It's available, it gives, it energizes, and it exists as an invitation rather than a declaration.

Engaging with powerful people can be complex because oftentimes, if we were abused, we were abused by people operating in power-over and/or power-to. This can grow into a very real fear of power, of powerful people, and especially fear of our own power. It's so easy to believe that power really does corrupt people, especially when we look at what corrupt people do with power.

One unexpected but unsurprising effect of this is that we're trained at a young age to deny our own power. If everyone used all of their power for

> Society corrupts, but power is nothing more than potential energy.

the highest good, the oppressive systems in this world that depend on people's compliance would crumble. We're often encouraged to be selfless, *as though that's a good thing*. What people usually mean when they say "selfless" is charitable and generous, but they don't use those words; they say "selfless." That didn't naturally just start happening. To be selfless is literally to be without a self, and if your personhood cup isn't full of your essence, it's that much easier for others to fill you with expectations of you, their wants and desires for your time, and their priorities for your energy. Conversely, what do people say when you unapologetically claim your power and acknowledge your best attributes or most impactful accomplishments? They say you're "full of yourself" *as though that's a bad thing*. Everywhere we turn in this society, we are programmed (largely by each other) to make ourselves small and not use our power. We're taught that if we use power, we're corrupt. If we acquire power, we're evil.

Ego

Our society has corrupted the word "ego," and many people have defined it through the lens of it being the bad parts of us, the part of us that needs healing, or the part of us that we need to kill if we are to be spiritual. Our ego is the vehicle through which we can experience being here. It is the emotional, experiential, motivational, goal-seeking part of us that we need to have fun here and engage on earth in a body! If we are abused, depressed, and slowly disavow ourselves of our ego and right to be here, as we shrink in shame and fear, we slowly quit living. This leads to suicidal ideation. Someone who doesn't care to be here anymore has lost sight of their ego and motivation to live deeply and fully, go after goals, and be here fully. They are the opposite of that.

As we heal and as Amanita helps us go inside and find our divinity, one of the first things we feel is how big we are and how amazing it is to be here; we feel a strong motivation to go do things. We start to become the opposite of a small ego; we start to grow our ego. Ego is not inherently bad. And saying we have to get rid of it usually comes from people trying to escape their own bodies using religion, spirituality, or psychology as an excuse to not feel or own who they are. They usually have issues with power and see themselves or others who own their power as arrogant and self-serving.

> *Our body is for our physical experiences of the space-time gravity plane. The ego is for our emotional and spiritual expression and experience.*

Narcissism

We should talk about narcissism for a second. It is a survival mechanism that's built into humans. We're born completely narcissistic as infants and 100% enmeshed in dependence. As we grow, we learn to develop a sense of self. At around 18 months, we start to begin our separation from our surroundings and our caregivers. Around three, we fully start to see them as separate individuals and start to test those boundaries. In doing that, we learn about loving others and loving ourselves. As we grow and develop, we begin to understand friendship and how to set boundaries and respect other people's boundaries. As our world expands and we grow up safely in a healthy environment, we learn to value others and ourselves. This continues to unfold until around age 23 to 25, when we develop a global awareness and the ability to think symbolically in higher-ordered states.

However, if something happened to you even as a healthy adult and you were brutalized for a year of your life, you would become narcissistic. By necessity, that is your body's way of protecting you and making sure your needs get met. It's challenging to think about other people when you're in survival mode and bombarded with flashbacks, triggers, and trauma.

The way out of that would be therapy, to relearn about boundaries–how yours were violated and how you've violated those of others. Narcissism is when you're unable to consider anyone else's experiences but your own, so it's common for people suffering from abuse and abusive systems to be temporarily narcissistic.

That could either look like asking someone you trust if they're willing to support you through this process or simply isolating a little so you can take care of yourself, clean up your diet, get a movement practice going, and go to therapy and use entheogens and integration. In addition, it could be helpful to exercise discretion in your conversations, making sure not to railroad them by talking about yourself too much. Pull back from those social circles until you can consistently hold a healthy amount of space for others.

The goal here is to strike that balance of setting boundaries with toxic people while you are growing and changing rapidly and not being in a narcissistic state while you do this work. You're learning to embrace who you are and grow out of narcissism into new, higher, better, more enlightened spaces. If you have been worried about your selfishness or levels of behavior toward others, I hope this part of this chapter helps shed some light on it. The balance is owning your power over self, owning your goodness, and also owning your shame and narcissism while you learn to grow into your new places.

> If you notice people setting a lot of boundaries with you or pulling away, seek the input of a mental health professional.

Owning Your Power

If you keep taking Amanita, you won't have a choice but to continue to power up. Even if you're not trying to, you will do it, and it will push people's buttons for a myriad of reasons. Understand that they are responsible for their own buttons. Some people will be triggered because they've been hurt by powerful people before; if you step into your power, they may fear you'll hurt them too. Others can be triggered because they know they're not standing in their power, and your powerlessness was validating them.

These are the people who will say, "You've changed," *as though that's not what we're here to do*.

Still, others will be triggered because they're jealous, as though this kind of power is something that can be earned, acquired, transferred, lost, or stolen. These are the people who will try to turn the tables and find a way to exert power over you, to either make you question your own power, or feed their need to feel power over others.

Understand that the power I'm talking about–the power you'll be stepping into–is an internal power. It's feeling larger and stronger, and owning the space you take up on the planet. If you feel different in this way, then you were smaller before.

> *The more power you have over yourself, the less room there is for others to have power over you.*

That's a problem for people who want to have power over you. The more self-governing you are, the more you see your divinity, your birthright, and your sovereignty, the harder it will be for others to manipulate you. This is a problem for those who want to. So the power the Amanita will invite you to reclaim isn't power you can wield over others or take from them, and it's not a power anyone can take from you. It was always yours. They're just showing you it's there and giving you permission to step back into it.

There's a reason I'm talking about this after establishing the importance of shifting from black-and-white thinking to living in the in-between, moving from fear to love, and going from transactional relationships to freely giving ones and living through the heart. When you step into your power after making all of these shifts, you will be an unstoppable force for the good of humanity. This is where the Amanita is working to bring you. It's just this amazing and beautiful package where you get power and love at the same time. Power plus discernment plus love is good.

A New Way of Being

One of the things that you may start to notice is your mannerisms. Try not to force yourself into old mannerisms. If you do something unusual, you can notice that it's different and new, but do everything you can not to judge the new thing as bad, wrong, or out of character. Technically, you're supposed to be out of character because you've been playing a character this whole time, and the Amanita has slowly been helping you outgrow that like an old sweater.

If you're standing in the kitchen, and you suddenly feel the need to widen your stance and strike a power pose. Do it!

You'll find that instead of saying:

> I'm sorry to bother you,

you'll say:

> **Thank you for taking my call.**

Instead of:

> Sorry for wasting your time,

you'll say:

> **Thank you for your time.**

You'll carry yourself as though you deserve the things you're asking for, and that will be coupled with only asking for what you need. When you're pitching a collaboration or partnership, it won't be, "Hey do you think we could partner on this thing?" Instead, it will be, "Here's what I'm up to on my own, and here's where I think our work will fit nicely together. Let's take this to the next level together." People will start saying yes to you less because of what you're asking them to say yes to and more because of the confidence and drive they feel in your energy.

Time to Power Up

To be what the earth needs you to be, this is what you're going to have to eventually own. This is what you've got to present yourself with. And I can tell you right now, this earth needs you. Look at the world the way it is right now, and tell me we don't need good people doing powerful things. How are you going to get them done? By being powerful. By knowing that power can be a force for good.

Can you tolerate the anger? Can you tolerate the grieving? Because you've got to get through those things before you can power up. Can you say yes? Personally, this has been the longest, most difficult "yes experiment" of my life, and it's been going on for years. The Amanita keeps saying, "Cool. You stepped up to the next platform. Will you say yes to this next one?" And it's always a terrifying step to take. I'll say, "Yes, thank you, Amanita. Can I have another?" "Yes, thank you, Amanita. Can I have another?" And every time I say "yes," I'm terrified. I always wind up in a whole new type of terrifying, and I just keep marching forward. Now, if I look back on what was terrifying me two years ago, it's something I do easily now.

THIS IS HOW WE POWER UP.

Power can be beautiful, and power can be good, and what you will notice is that instead of feeling like you occupy this really thin line inside your body, or you only occupy this tiny spot inside your heart, or you only occupy the space inside your head, you will start to notice that you fully feel like you occupy your whole body. You will slowly start expanding into more and more parts of your body.

You get to move back into your liver again. You get to move back into your stomach again. You get to move back into your knees. Any part of your body where you hold resistance, anywhere that's holding pain and shame, you get to reoccupy it. And before you know it, you are aware of your feet on the ground, and you are aware of the top of your head, and you feel divinity in your hands. Next, you will start to realize you are occupying space outside your body. And then you will start to realize you are showing up way out there before your physical body shows up. And that's when strangers will start walking up to you on the street, not even realizing they are walking toward you. And then that opens up a whole new can of worms in regards to setting boundaries. People will smile at you more and sometimes just ask if you need their help or how they can become involved in whatever it is you are doing. And if you are involved in outreach and passion projects, you will need that.

Power As Energy

As you power up, your body will start to tune itself to optimize. The equipment you're using, you will use better. You will become more efficient. Things work faster and better. You feel better. You are lighter. You will solve a problem before there's a real problem, with creativity that will seem magical. You're dealing with your toxicity. You're improving your mood, and you're improving your motivation. The more you do the work, the more you identify as someone who's growing and changing and shedding old things that no longer work for you.

At the end of the day, it all comes back to love. Love yourself as enthusiastically as you'd love a good friend. Be your biggest cheerleader and remind yourself how enriched humanity would be if you shared your gifts with them. And then remember that your greatest gift is love. Your mission statement, your "big why," has to have love at the center. So love yourself enough to step into your power unapologetically. Love others enough to use your power for good.

It starts with you, and the world needs what you have to offer.

CHAPTER 20 — Anger

Before we approach this chapter, please know that we are discussing lower levels of anger which can be persistent or spike periodically. If you are having difficulty or if you are acting out, it is important to seek help from a professional.

Sometimes it can be surprising and unnerving when we start to feel this level of anger with Amanita. We might be tempted to think we've done something wrong, taken too much, must not be very spiritual, or are somehow regressing. When this first happened to me, it was really upsetting. I would go on to learn that I had a lot of anger and that it was justified. I had temporarily believed the spiritual world's claims that anger means you aren't spiritual or that you're being egoic. Ha!

Indeed, anger is the part of you that loves you. It is the most profoundly loving part of yourself trying to get your attention.

Anger is a most welcome sign that you are reaching your inner self, which has been shoved down for far too long. Anger is a gift. Loving yourself, waking up to your inner wisdom, and finally opening that vault is the most spiritual thing you could be doing right now. So, if you are experiencing anger and it is scaring you, I hope you can relax and take it as it comes. I hope you will welcome it as the harbinger of good things on the way.

Boundary Violations

When you first start taking Amanita, that anger could be telling you, you have said "yes" to bullshit for far too long, to the point where you have become complacent in your own oppression. You have said "no" to the things you needed in your life just to appease your oppressors. You have shoved down your inner voice until it went silent. You have a lot to be angry about, and you'll discover that most, if not all, of them were boundary violations. Times you didn't set boundaries because you were never taught how or that you could, and yet felt violated anyway. Times you did set boundaries, and they were ignored or steamrolled. Times you were punished for even setting them in the first place.

Betrayal trauma is another way we have developed unresolved anger. If we were promised things by adults and then they just didn't do it, forgot, said they never made that promise, never showed up, or left us unable to trust anyone's word anymore, the betrayal becomes 'the way people are,' and we normalize it and excuse it. Eventually, the anger we feel seems ridiculous, so we shove it down in our adult lives as us being unreasonable because this is just how people are. When this happens on a daily basis in childhood, weekly in adulthood, multiplied by how many years, it's no wonder that one of the early things to surface, asking to be addressed, is anger.

Mushrooms are incredibly matter-of-fact. We learn on this mushroom that none of this is normal. None of this is okay. One of the beautiful things about Amanita is that it goes through the heart, and so yes, you may feel that anger and that rage, but you may not know where to put it because it's just coming up as free-floating anger. Because these things have been normalized, you likely weren't keeping score when every injury happened. But your body was. So you'll feel emotions attached to events you don't remember. *Don't gaslight yourself* and tell yourself these feelings aren't valid. They are.

> As anger is the advocacy emotion, you can understand why anger will bubble up as you come to these realizations.

Right now, loving yourself comes in the form of giving yourself what your caregivers didn't give you growing up: permission to express yourself fully and truly. If you experience random free-floating anger, loving yourself right now seems like allowing that anger room to move on out and set itself free. Liberating something stuck, like anger, is the most gracious act of self-love you can be doing right now. Imagine how much lighter you are going to feel when you can move that stuck energy out. Find outlets for that anger anywhere you can that are safe for you and others.

Where (And Where Not) to Channel Your Anger

If you get on social media during this period of your journey, you will find places where you will feel like you need to advocate for people. Let me just say, this is not the time for that. If you are used to feeling for others, then your reaction to anger might be to feel empathy and outrage for injustice online. This reaction needs to inform you and be an alarm bell for you. You need to use your energy wisely right now, and throwing it up randomly all over the internet to rescue people who aren't being heard in comment sections is not the way to use this energy. Don't do it. Stay off of social media. When you feel the anger, just get off and walk away.

Anger is your body's way of getting your attention. It's as if physical pain were an emotion. It's just your body saying, "Hey, you need to address this thing, right here, right now." You may not be able to put your finger on it at first, but the more you lean in with curiosity and openness, the more the memories will start to surface. Random free-floating anger can be very troubling indeed. But allow this part. Allow anger that has no direction. Allow it to feel uncomfortable without trying to direct it. When you point it outward, working to find who is oppressing you or someone else right now it is blocking the true reason for this moment of anger.

> Behind all that anger is the sadness, the grieving, and the hurt.

I was six years old on the playground, and pieces from the necklace I made were falling all over the ground as the boy who yanked it off my neck ran away laughing, holding it in the air like a victory flag. I sat down to cry, and the teacher came over to console me, saying she would talk to both of our parents about it. Nothing ever happened. Life went on, and all I was left with was a broken necklace, a boundary violation that no one did anything about, and a message that the time and effort I put into making it was worthless, and therefore *I* was worthless. Today, all I did was pick up a handmade necklace I was given when suddenly I felt anger, which turned into tears. This is the power of anger and healing today.

This period lasted about nine months for me. As you move through this chapter, just have grace for yourself and for what you're moving through as you are slowly owning your power. Take this to your therapy. Recognizing your abuse, feeling the anger and sadness, allowing it a voice, and moving into your power, is a process. You're going to get to a place where you are very big. Remember Alice, the potion that makes her big and small. This is Amanita. Allow her room to do the work. And allow that anger is part of the process of healing. While you may deal with the bulk of it in this stage, don't be surprised when anger shows up every time you approach the entheogens.

> *The goal is to learn to recognize anger as one of the first things to show up each time you move into a new area of growth, asking, learning, and healing.*

Being an advocate during the anger phase is not a good idea. At some point, you will be coming back into advocacy if that is where you are called to work, but you will probably see that you are doing it in a whole new way from a completely different space inside yourself. Anger is not a position of power. Anger is sadness, and is vulnerable. It's a time of work on self. Later, you can work for others.

I hear you. I see your compassion, love, and empathy for others–especially when you see yourself in them and you see them suffering the very same trespasses and violations you experienced. You know their plight and feel uniquely qualified to empathize, understand, and protect them. This is all true, and during the anger phase of your Amanita journey, stepping in will likely only be like adding oil to an already blazing fire. This phase will pass, and you'll find your footing again and be able to tackle these things with power, but not necessarily force. And you'll understand that difference later as you grow to embody it. Now is the time to sit with your own anger, be with your own feelings about the things you personally have suffered, and do your healing work within.

> The world needs your power. But before you can step into it, you have to deal with the anger that the Amanita will raise in you.

You have a lot of reasons to be angry just by being a human, and the more the Amanita works with you, the more your eyes will be open to the things you have to be angry about, and the more you'll learn how to express your emotions in healthy ways. The hope is that all who see these injustices will use them to open more doors for others and hold them open. One of the beautiful things that's happening with technology and social media is indigenous people and people of color, and people in marginalized communities are getting platforms, and their voices are being heard like never before. And the more doors we can hold open for each other, the more all of us are going to continue to increase our power at this table. It's what the Earth is asking of all of us. This new world where we all can live and breathe in peace together is going to require making room for each other at that table. If someone opens a door, go hold it. If someone brings a gift through that door, pick it up and help spread it out. Whatever your gift is, whatever it is you want to do, you're going to have to start in your heart and deal with the anger first.

CHAPTER 21 — *Boundaries*

> Before we get into this, *make sure you know what boundaries are*. They are not used to control other people, force actions, or punish. Boundaries are how we move away, protect the self, and stay in our space. If you are unsure about boundaries, a mental health professional can help.

One side effect of stepping into your power is that you start attracting lots of attention. People just inexplicably gravitate toward you, and then you have to start saying "no" in a whole different way. As it turns out, the less self-sovereignty someone has, the more they'll be attracted to you. The less of their own power they've stepped into, the more they'll want to bask in yours.

Remember the anxiety I talked about, the government time I talked about, the rigidity, the fear, and the black-and-white thinking? Now that you're stepping out of those things and can see them clearly, you'll see them at play in the majority of people who flock to you when you start to stand in your power. People will want help, they'll want answers, they'll want guidance, they'll want mentorship, they'll want protection, they'll want a new parent or big sibling, or a good influence for their kids. These wants take a large amount of energy to provide, wield, and give intelligently.

None of this is your job. If you're an average joe like the rest of us, a lot of the things people will come to you for will be things you're not fully qualified to give. In a weird way, saying "yes" to yourself and your own growth and evolution often means learning to say "no" to people who want to ride your wave to circumvent the life lessons in their own world.

I am not saying you can't help others. I am saying that going through your own fire of the shadow work and the darkness, the energy you've spent, and the things you've lost, have cost you. The work you are doing to find your power, what it looks like, how it feels, how to hold it, how to wield it, and the toll it takes when you choose to give it, will cause you to realize you can no longer just act willy nilly, in how you show up to the world.

> *The price you pay for owning your power is knowledge that your energy is finite, and now you must choose carefully how and when you spend it.*
>
> *And that choice is holy.*

That choice is one of the most personal, honorable, and respectful things any human can do. Once you realize this, you will also see that for others. How someone chooses to spend their time, their knowledge, their helping is the most high and sacred of things in humanness.

Say Goodbye to Smallness

This is what Amanita is going to ask you to work through. If you tend to make excuses and just give what people are asking of you, saying, "Oh, it's not worth it. I don't like confrontation anyway. That's okay. I don't mind. They can have it," you are draining your energy, allowing boundary violations, and you are leaking. Amanita is going to ask you to take ownership of your choices. You can't make any more excuses for your behavior. You're going to need to own and take accountability for it and start pointedly putting your energy out there specifically, with awareness. If you just sling that motivation and energy out everywhere and let whoever grabs it grab it, you're going to spin your wheels, and you're going to get hurt, be used, drained, taken advantage of, and that will cost you, you.

This is your power. And your power requires your attention. Your power requires you to own your love, your beauty, your divinity, and your ego. Look at yourself and ask yourself, 'What means the most to me? How can I be a force for good? What is darkness? What is love? Am I what people tell me I am?' As you begin to change and start thinking before helping, you will set boundaries and start saying "no." People might call you cold-hearted and say you don't care. The more you own your power, the more people might call you arrogant and egotistical. The more this happens, the more of a reputation you might start to build for yourself. And being Amanita Dreamer, now, going through this on a large scale, I have a new way of seeing this.

There are people in the world who spend their energy focused inward, working to be a better person. There are people who are focused on helping the world heal. Then there are people focused on worrying about how they can get resources from others, tear them down, and spend their energy working to spread their disdain. Instead of questioning people who are working to do good, I question the people who hate them.

When you begin to experience people being hateful to you, then starting to spread lies about you, this is when you have to realize you've made some headway into your growth. This is when you need to make hard choices about not caring what others think so that you can spend your energy working on how to allow others to hate you. This is the beginning of being an asshole for some people.

Know yourself. Are you? Maybe you are. Maybe you're an asshole using entheogens to parade as a good person. Maybe you're a narcissist, and you're here just to learn how to be a better narcissist. If you are having issues with stepping into your power, please see your mental health professional so you can find how to land in this.

There's a reason I saved this for the end of the book. This is the graduation. This is why you really picked up this book. Everything up to this point was to get you here. This is the point of all these entheogens and all this work—not to escape your ego, not to quit having feelings, not to feel happy all the time, but to live in your own body fully and love it while you enjoy the experience here.

Own your divinity. Find your reason for being here, and do that thing so you can finally say, "I have no regrets. I did it. I did the thing I came here to do." That's what power is, and we need you. Now. All of the humans being born right now need you to build the construct they can walk onto and make the changes they're going to have the power to make.

It's All Connected

When I told you in the beginning, "Wherever you feel resistance, learn how to let that go and learn how to lean in," do you see now that wherever you're feeling resistance, and you lean in, and you feel it, and then you let that emotion go, how easy it is for love to take its place? Do you see how important it is for that love to sit beside your power so that you can live through your heart? It's all connected. Remember how we need to flow, because rushing is violence? And remember how you need to flow so that you can allow things to work as they're meant to so that when you do that thing, you create reciprocity, which then creates movements, which then creates this world that you want to inhabit?

This is how it all comes together.

This is what I've been building up to. This is where I was taking you. When people talk about taking mushrooms and *only* tripping, when people talk about manifesting and *only* manifesting, when people talk about therapy and *only* therapy, when people talk about learning to trust yourself and *only* learning to trust yourself, the reason why it doesn't seem to work is that they're only looking at one piece of a much larger puzzle. And the missing piece for most people today is the use of these entheogens with integration. Now that we've got the entheogens, there's this new conversation around how to use them and what they do. People want to talk about them like they are their own separate thing, but they're not. The conversation about psychology and therapy and reparenting and trauma healing, the conversation about energy healing and manifesting and celestial timing, and the conversation about entheogens and ancient plant-based wisdom and practices—these are all the same conversation.

Know Your Value

I've already talked about this indirectly in this chapter, but I'm going to name it and say it explicitly. Where you're headed, the Universe is going to bring you experiences that feel dreamy and make you think, "There's no way I deserve this." I'm here to tell you that you do. You always have. It was your birthright, your divinity, human tools we have all always been born with. The voices in your head telling y ou you're undeserving are the old programs, old habits, and old traumas that this mushroom will help you shed like old skin.

Allowing others to just give to me freely has been the hardest part of this so far. All this work has been hard, and growing into this space of owning my power has felt like my passion and something that felt like the next right phase of my development. But the most daunting part has been allowing love to flow back to me. Realizing I have value outside of what I can do for others has been the greatest and latest thing in my growth. And maybe you find this inside you too.

My good friend Travis who held space for me with the mushrooms while I screamed and worked for 3 or 4 hours told me, "Just say thank you". I felt so apologetic for all that noise and for being troublesome. And he just loved me and kept saying, "Just say thank you". He didn't abandon me later, when his offering was over. We continue to work together in different ways of advocacy, helping others and our paths crossing. He doesn't treat me like I'm less than for having witnessed the ugly. Many people take from me and in return for reciprocity, give things back. But there are times when people just give, deeply, not having taken anything from me. Others want to express gratitude for what I have freely given them. Stepping into your value and divinity will be a graduation that might be surprisingly challenging. Giving is easy, if it is how you've shown up and earned your worth, allowing others to give what you need might be a hard new road to walk.

Your Value In Service

Asking a fair price for your labor and being paid for it with no questions asked might feel startling and like surely you don't deserve this. Valuing our beingness, allowing love to flow into us, allowing others with resources to show up and give them, asking for what it will take for you to show up and allowing others to pay it gladly are graduations. Let me ask you this. If your dreams involve land, or a building or hand outs to serve a community, how are you going to pay for those things? How are you going to acquire those things? If you don't own them now, you MUST be able to bring in more than you currently do. You need to eat, have a home and have your life in order, in order to raise everything up to a level where you are now also bringing in the things you need to create the world you want to create.

An animal rescue requires an incredible number of resources, grants, infrastructure, and people. The things that you want to do for the world means that you will need more things, paperwork, advice, professional help, gifts of service and technology. You will need easy money to grab when the time is right, you need safety and support. When all these things begin to flow in, when people see your love and passion project and they see your vision too, and they want to help, they will. When the scales tip and things just begin flowing, it can feel overwhelming. You become a conductor of an orchestra, of power, money, people and things swooshing in. And it will require you to be able to stand firmly in your power, assuredness and ability to keep it moving while watching this new thing build and watching the happiness on others faces.

Whatever it is, that you envision for your joy filled life, how you want to give to the world and feel useful, to get that requires that you step fully into your value and power and divinity. If you do, you will find yourself in your dream life watching it serve those you wanted to serve and helping in the way you wanted to. Discernment, love, acceptance, giving, reciprocity, saying yes, wielding energy, attracting the right people at the right time, the love and feeling deserving of it, are the graduation of all of this.

As you grow and as your vision grows and as your abilities grow, it attracts others who feel called to be working in this arena, on the construct you are building. They are making their dreams come true also. They wake up feeling excited about showing up for you to play their part in this thing. How will it serve all of it, if you aren't taking the lead and making decisions? If you don't ask for what you need, if you are only allowing yourself to be paid exactly the minimum you need to get by, how will this serve you, your dreams and the entire thing you want to build, and those who want to be part of it and those who will be the recipients of it?

Even if you just want a quiet house in the woods and a few animals, you will still need resources to get it and the ability to establish boundaries to protect your space. From the small to the large, helping others, to living your dream, knowing your value is at the core of it.

We live in a world where money and time are exchanged so often people have started saying they're one and the same. So as you start to learn your value, and how to value your work–whether that's setting an hourly wage you want to make, determining what you feel your annual income should be, or even pricing things you've made like products or art–start by asking what your time is worth to you. Your worth is what you believe you're worth. What does it take for you not to be lying in bed, scrolling through your favorite thing, knitting, doing your craft, or being out hiking–whatever your joy is? What would it cost for somebody to tear you away from that? That's what you're worth. Whatever that's going to cost to take you away from your children. Pack your stuff up, kiss your animals goodbye, and get in an airplane and go to them. What's that worth to you?

Sometimes, saying "no" to giving time and energy, and solutions to a friend in a bind is the most loving thing you can do because as long as they have someone to bail them out, life will never be hard enough to motivate them to figure out how to do it on their own. I'm not saying this is always the case with everyone. You just need to be discerning about the best way for you to love people. Sometimes that means saying, "Yes, I love you, and I will help you with whatever you need," and other times, that will mean saying, "No, I love you, and I'm choosing to spend my energy elsewhere." And that's okay.

> *The world needs whatever it is you are passionate about. The world needs you.*

Can you imagine moving this many parts, where you've finally met your dreams only to come home to a mess, clutter and piles of things that don't belong anymore? Can you imagine coming home to someone who is jealous and hateful to you daily? Can you imagine doing this while also having to put weeks in between to stop and deal with your bullshit because all along this path you refused to do it? Can you imagine doing this work while you cuss and complain, driving fast and rushing everywhere?

Every part of this book has addressed important parts of this growth. Using equinoxes and solstices and what they require in getting rid of things that no longer serve, when they require working, creating, growth and expansion, you are doing the work of growth, shadow work, self-work, love work. When you became flow, when you replaced rigidity with rituals, when you did the next right thing in this path, you slowly built yourself to a place where you have stability and value. Entheogens can be their own fun thing, but many people think just taking them is all there is. And it can be. But work comes after. The work is what this book is about. The graduation is watching it come together outside of you in a world of dreams and you are building it.

Step into your power, know your value, and what you're capable of. Set out to make that mark. This will mean partnering with new people, going into new spaces you feel unqualified to be in, venturing into saying yes, and being treated with respect. It will mean being seen and asked to fill roles that make you feel lucky and happy. If you want to be able to say yes to all of these opportunities, you will need the available energy to do so. You can't afford to leak energy. In this power, you will wield energy. You will become a magical wizard. And this makes you a person of the mushroom; magical, powerful, and dreamy.

Family reunion

CHAPTER 22

High Dosing

> While beautiful and indeed truly healing, I want to say upfront that high dosing is not the way to use this mushroom the first time or even in the early stages of using it.

Having said that, let's talk about high doses.

High dosing Amanita muscaria, unlike psilocybin mushrooms, is not a simple dosing guideline. As a matter of fact, the higher you dose, the more varying the issues become with dosing. Take into consideration that there are two medicines at play here.

With Amanita, using both medicines together, we get increasing opportunities for growth and expansion with a lot of safety built in. With ibotenic acid being a more playful side and muscimol being a more hard-hitting side, using both creates a balance and an easier way to deal with what can be very deep issues. For this reason, using the tea recipe and continuing to advance with its use is the proper route to go with high dosing. After maxing out on the tea by reaching your limit of ibotenic acid, the next step is to shift to a full muscimol conversion.

With both, as you get to higher doses, you will need to have a sitter with you. This is not an experience or medicine you can do at high doses without help. This is also not a medicine where you define what you think a high dose should be and then jump into that dose. High doses are amazing and valuable experiences.

Getting there, however, should be progressive.

I spent the first year with Amanita slowly increasing my tea dose. In the second year, I began working with higher doses of tea. In the third year, I started working with the milk conversion method and did the first dose on camera which you can view on AmanitaDreamer.net. After that, I worked my way into higher doses with it. At five years of Amanita use, only in the past year have I been doing doses where I needed to have help. They have been integral to my healing. Getting here took years.

In this chapter, I will teach you how to slowly progress through these stages. I do so with the continued warnings that you should not jump into any stage of this without working your way there. I also do this with the warnings about using a sitter in the areas where I tell you below. I am not saying this to be cautious or to cover myself publicly. I say this because this is how it is. People rarely have good outcomes if they jump into high doses of either the tea or the full conversion.

Tea High Dosing

After you feel good about your experiences with macrodosing, you can start to work into your higher doses. To do this, you will use the tea method and add lemon to it every time you use it. If you continue to increase your dose and you reach a point where you get nauseous or crampy, that is your indication that you need more conversion. This is ibotenic acid letting you know. If this is the case, simmer the tea longer, about another 15 minutes, then add lemon to whatever you are taking, giving it a few minutes for the chemistry to happen for the low pH acid to convert more. Early studies I'm doing with chemists are showing that most of the conversion will happen in the first hour and that little conversion happens without low pH.

Each time you push your dose of the tea higher, simmer it a little longer, add lemon, and keep going. When you reach a point where you are simmering it for an hour and adding lemon, and you are getting cramps or nausea, *you have reached your personal limit of high-dosing the tea*. At this point, if you wish to continue with higher doses, you have reached a hallmark in your work with Amanita. This took me several years.

Muscimol

From here, the next step is muscimol conversion. As of the writing of this book, even after a few decades of study, there is very little conclusive science on using a boil method to fully convert. Currently, it looks like very low pH with heat is the most important method if you have to use water only.

The methods that we know work use lactobacillus bacteria for a full and complete conversion. This method has the science behind it, which started with the Trent Austin patent. That continued with him and Kevin Feeney discussing the possibility of raw milk in Kevin's Fly Agaric book. See the References section at the back of the book for information on these pieces of literature.

After speaking with Kevin Feeney, I experimented with raw milk from a local dairy and got a full conversion since raw milk has this bacteria in it naturally. You can also buy yogurt starter and add it to store-bought milk, since the starter has this bacteria.

There is also a vegan method using a ferment with the naturally occurring lactobacillus on ginger. The method works, but you will need patience, time, and the correct tools. The first step uses a ginger bug to grow the bacteria, and the second step puts the Amanita tea with the bacteria for the ferment/conversion. I have had less success putting the whole mushroom in it. These recipes can be found on AmanitaDreamer.net.

The other option is to allow your sitter to be a shaman who works with this mushroom to make it for you and guide your experience. As of the writing of this book, there are very few who do this. I will be working diligently to find them as this information grows and spreads. I have a page on the website devoted to practitioners where you can locate someone. I will continue to grow that page.

Yet another other option is to attend a group ceremony where you can enter into an experience with this mushroom with others doing the same.

To create a few barriers of entry into high-dosing muscimol, I am not going to lay out step-by-step instructions in this book. I don't want to create instructions for impulsive people to share and use to cause harm.

Once you have your full conversion, which I will call SOMA for ease of reference, you are ready to begin the same process all over again that you used with the tea. Start small and see how you react to muscimol. Using a premade product for microdosing muscimol is a good way to see how it makes you feel. If you want to go with higher doses, then you can use the conversion you made to work with small doses and become familiar with it. When you reach a dose where you have difficulty walking, you are reaching a point where you should not be alone. And I will note here, that when you reach that range, accidentally going over to the point where you lose the ability to control yourself can be a small margin.

> Muscimol is not something to fear. It is to be respected.

If you start small and work your way up, you will become familiar with the area where you begin to be at the edge of that control. If you have used alcohol, you are aware of these states, from being buzzed to drunk to complete blackout but still up and around to passing out. Using muscimol at the edge is where you will be making the choices to work with someone versus working alone. Keep in mind that line is easy to cross. Some people do it and are fine the next day without harm, and others hurt themselves.

How Does Muscimol Cause Harm?

The harm with muscimol is that it works by creating a space where you are both dreaming and awake. Whether or not it actually changes your brainwaves, I don't yet know, but I am working on that. To me, it feels like lower alpha brainwaves, like early sleep. I dip in and out of awareness. Once you fall deeply into the trip state, you can look asleep to others, but you can also "wake up" and walk around and talk and move, but you are still in the sleep state like sleepwalking. You can act out the trip you are experiencing, which is how people harm themselves. This is why a sitter is necessary. In my experimenting with this to help create more information and harm reduction, I went to this state without help and got serious burns on my face because I tried to cook while deeply in the trip experience. Another time I fell down the stairs.

The issues were that I time traveled to points where the food was still cold while it was hot and cooking. I traveled ahead where I reached the bottom of the stairs while I was still at the top of the stairs. Time travel is a prominent feature of this mushroom at all stages of use.

The other issue is that you can put yourself in dangerous places or situations, like being outside in subfreezing temperatures. If you are in a warm house in your trip, that's where you'll believe you are, even if you are slowly freezing outside. A sitter will help you stay seated or in bed, and keep you safe.

When I have held a ceremony, even with warnings for people to be careful and not use high doses, some still do. They usually need constant care. Some become angry and act out scenarios and need to be held down by several people. Sitters need to be capable in this capacity. Great healing has come from these experiences by these people and others using high doses. It must happen with great care.

There are reasons why many people don't like this mushroom, and I believe this is the number one reason. The other reason for the dislike or for the negative stories is that people have jumped into high muscimol doses without ever having used this mushroom before. They went by bad advice for high doses and wound up sick and in the hospital. This is very high overdosing and is completely avoidable.

The "start small and work your way up" advice is the reason most people won't ever advise it and won't give help about dosing it. Something this complex doesn't usually go over well with a public who want distilled sound bites and simple instructions. This mushroom doesn't work that way. Therefore, this mushroom is not for those people.

Don't fear it. It is a beautiful medicine. The healing in it is indescribable.

This is not a race. Taking your time through this journey gives real, lasting healing. Expect to spend a few years with this medicine as you slowly deepen your relationship together. As you do, you will grow and learn about it in such deep and profound ways that it will leave you with gratitude that is also indescribable. You meet elders and ancestors. You meet other places and times and lifetimes. You learn esoteric things that you won't bring home with you, but you will have integrated into yourself without the knowledge of how they got there. You can integrate indescribable levels of being that affect all parts of your life, but which you cannot find words to enunciate what it is or why you know it. Connection to intuition, higher knowledge, and downloads happen in a mystical place that you won't remember.

The awakening and profundity in how you see the world, the depth of yourself and creation that you can find are indescribable and are far beyond just stopping anxiety and panic. I condone high doses. But I do so with all of the cautions here. I do so with the warnings that it takes time. I do so with the limits of your knowing yourself and this medicine deeply so that it can inform your progress.

Start small with the tea and work your way up. Start small with muscimol and work your way up. Get help when you journey and take all the time you need between doses to integrate. Each time you increase your dose and journey, you need a long time to integrate. What I have written about in this book only becomes more pronounced with higher doses.

> *The higher your dose, the longer integration takes and the more fearful it can become.*

As you do this, you will learn what the fear means, and how to ride it out and work with it. As you work with this, you will reach higher states of consciousness that may make it more difficult to cope. You may need to put a lot of down-time inbetween high doses, just to learn how to live in society as you change.

I realize this chapter doesn't leave you many options. We are still very early in the modern stages of using the mushroom. We are slowly relearning this. And as of now, this is just the current landscape. The lack of good information coupled with bad information along with fear-mongering with publicized bad experiences create a paradigm where moving forward here requires discernment. My goal with this chapter is to simply give you information about moving forward *on your own*. I am not building the framework for that here. I hope in the future, we see that framework built with many places for you to find healing. I hope to be involved in that.

My suspicion is that you will judge this however you will, then the mushroom voice will have you wanting, curious, asking, and seeking. Don't be surprised if you feel like this is too risky, only to find yourself with a microdose, then a macrodose, then pushing that upward. That is how it should be. Slow. Steady. Comfortable.

Your First High Dose

Imagine a place, whether real or imaginary, in which you feel completely safe, at peace, and could stay for years without getting tired of it. Now imagine you have an opportunity to spend a week there with an old sage teacher, and you would have their undivided attention for the duration of the week.

Hold this image as you answer the following questions.

WORKSHEET #8: Your First High Dose

Write down the first thing you would ask the Sage Teacher.

Write down some things you'd hope the two of you would do together.

Imagine it's the end of the week. What do you hope that you have gained, learned, and now understand?

Modern Western society tells us we need to look outside ourselves for answers. We're born into a man-made hierarchical societal format in which there are people above us and people below us. The implication is that we should learn from those above us and teach those below us. There's nothing inherently problematic about that, but when you couple it with the notion that "knowledge is power," suddenly, everyone on top of you gets to hold power over you. You probably think I'm going to start talking about how the answers are already inside you, and you need to look inward for the wisdom you seek. That's not untrue, but it's actually not what I'm leading up to.

I asked you to answer those questions to prepare you for your first higher dose so that you can begin to practice realizing that you're not a passenger in the experience. You are going to this place to visit an ancient wise elder. And I want you to begin to understand that practice of setting your intention. What do you want to ask them? What do you want to know? So when they show up in your space, you'll have an idea of what to do.

This is not a made-up scenario. It's not an allegory or metaphor. You will literally go do this.

Take what you wrote to your session and to the wisdom you find there. And continue to do this every time to prepare for macro and higher doses.

Now that we have done that, it's time to set a date for your first macrodose of muscimol. Choose a time when you have plenty of time to experiment. You may not get it on the first try. Finding your doses as you work your way up takes methodical patience. But at some point, sometimes on the first try, you will find that place. You will know it by the softness and love that creeps into your chest and the feeling that you are not alone. Check-in with the Elders and enjoy your discussions. Speak out loud or in your head the questions you have for them. Listen to the answers and have a recording device ready so you can take notes. You will learn through this process where to go next, how much to take, and how often you'd like to try higher doses. I did macrodoses frequently in the first two years. The boost in healing, learning, and growing is amazing. I hope you use this chapter as the declaration that it is time to move out of your comfort zone of microdosing and begin to push your edge into the higher wisdom of the mushroom.

Phases and what to expect

The Ibotenic Acid Muscimol Tea High Dose

The first phase of this will involve the highly active parts of ibotenic acid which you've grown used to. Having an activity planned, even if it is mundane like dishes, or just dancing, helps you move energy and emotions out of your body. It is part of the process so making plans for activity is very important. Going for a brisk walk is good but keep in mind that the ibotenic acid can change course suddenly so make sure you are close to home always.

Muscimol Phase 1

As it gives way to the muscimol side, you will start to travel in and out of being here. You may start to have the time jumps, the fracturing of reality and seeing time. When you close your eyes, you will start to feel like you are in space moving at speed. You may feel like you are wandering through your mind into dark parts of it or randomly having thoughts with no meaning or no connection to anything, freely floating disconnected. You may realize those thoughts are turning into voices outside of you. You may feel difficulty in your inner gut or heart area that you can't name or place. It may feel just "difficult" and hard to take. You might growl with the discomfort but naming it might be hard. Resist the urge to dismiss making sounds or vocalizing only because you can't find a physical reason for it, or you can't name an actual feeling. Being vocal is a very important part of this.

You may be here for a while in this space. When you come out of it you might be shocked to find it has only been 30 minutes. You may have new energy again and as this mushroom works in and out of your lessons, coming and going, tripping and then giving breaks, you will power down and in and power up and out. You will cycle like this for two or three hours before the big drop happens.

When muscimol takes over you will get very heavy, and you will know it is time to settle in. When it takes over you will likely still be up and talking but, in your memory, you went to sleep at that point. Your video or sitter will tell you that you were still awake and active. The early parts of muscimol are like that. This is the dangerous part of muscimol. The phase when it kicks in but before it makes you settle in deeply can be the sketchy part.

This is true if you are coming from the tea side and converting to muscimol on your trip or if you have taken only full conversion muscimol. High dose muscimol is the same.

As muscimol creeps in you will go in and out of consciousness, blipping from being aware you are walking in your hallway, to being just, gone. Not here. Not anywhere, just gone. You will return to yourself now standing in another room and no idea how you got there or where you've just been. The early phase of muscimol is like that. Active in your body, moving around acting out your trip while you come and go from conscious awareness of your present state of your body. As it deepens you may experience overlays of alternate realities from other times while you are currently looking at the present time in your home in front of you. You may experience being partly here while also partly in another time. This may look like another person from another time standing in your house while you talk to them. This will increase as muscimol takes over. Your overlays will deepen, your time gone will get longer. The extremes in time jumps will get longer. You may wind up in past lives completely, not even here in this one anymore. Each time you go, you get closer to the one where you don't come back but go deeply into a state of no longer being able to move around and your body will shut down and not move.

Keep this in mind as you move around. As you feel it deepen and as your time away gets longer, get yourself closer to the bed. You will probably feel it coming and will work your way there. But it can happen when you're new to this and don't know what to look for. It could happen while you are still in another room. So, try to create space on the floor in that room too just in case this is where you land and wind up for most of your journey.

Please keep in mind that this is very different from psilocybin. With higher doses of that, you eventually get to a point where your body won't work, and you can't move as you begin to leave this reality and go journey with the entities or wherever you go. The time when you leave tends to go along with not being able to move or walk. With muscimol in the early stages you will trip and leave while also acting it out physically. This is why it can be dangerous to not have someone with you.

Muscimol Phase 2

This part starts when your body goes quiet, and you aren't walking or talking anymore. If the work being done here is about age six and backward, keep in mind that much of your world was in your head. You lived in magical times, distorting the world around you. You lived in make believe and wonder. Things were new, you lived to play and learn. You wrote your memories very differently than you do today. Accessing those core memories requires access to a vault of experiences that happened in a very different way of recording life. It's much more mysterious but also recorded very deeply in your subconscious. If things that happened to you were deeply upsetting, it can be hard to open that vault. Even something as small as being the last kid picked up that day can feel very traumatizing to your 4-year-old self. If there were several kids in line and they were picked up in order and your caregiver was there but in the wrong place, trying to find you, for you, you were abandoned and forgotten. If your memories like this are all in this place spanning 6 years, that's a lot of trauma and stories and pain to access at once. In its grace, amanita says, "Go to sleep little one, we have work to do, and you don't need to see it all."

The mushroom is going in and breaking neurons, severing ties and emptying old memories and creating new ones, you will be living the trip. You will be interacting with entities who are working with you, soothing you, holding you down, watching you scream or cry or talking to you with a gentle hand. While this is happening, you look like you're sleeping very deeply. This is the amanita high dose muscimol trip. If you can remember or think about when new programs are installed on a computer, big updates on your phone, etc., it will load, shut down, turn back on, the screen will flash on and off and it may shut down again. This is what is happening while you are on a high dose muscimol trip. You are not asleep at all. A lot is happening but outside you seem asleep. For your memory it will feel like vivid intense dreaming or what some people will call lucid dreaming when in reality, it is a full-on trip. This is the deep inner work in the dark recesses of your inner core. In even higher doses or work that is very important and deeply tied, you may wind up going so deep you go out of the birth and backward in time to other lifetimes connected to this issue. You may find yourself living similar experiences in another time, place and with other people. The feelings and choices being very similar to today might be something you will recall later as you are integrating this experience. I have these memories as well. I became aware of past lives through this mushroom. I am aware of issues in this life that originated in others.

This work may result in you waking up and being conscious while the work is still going, the deep work happening, and you won't be able to move. Some people find this part upsetting. Being paralyzed but awake and aware is a possibility with this mushroom. I like the way it feels. It feels like, don't worry, nothing is expected of you so relax. Just breathe and let it work. Sit back and just be aware of how safe you are and how loved you are and how incredibly powerful this work is. Sit in your breathing, in and out, slowly while you lay here. I have a lot of experience with meditation, and I can't deny that may have an impact on how I react to this. Be aware that this is a possibility so that when it happens you can talk to yourself in it. Remember you can always talk to the mushroom. They love you. This part of the trip usually lasts for about 3 hours.

Muscimol Phase 3

Waking. It is common to wake up around 3 or 4 in the morning during this and feel excited and awake. For some, this is when the day starts. Or what may happen is you feel the energy and think that you want to get up and when you try, you can't. If that happens, you will usually go back in for round two of the previous stage. Waking up in between like this is common. Getting up or going back in is up to the mushroom. But once you wake up excited and get up, this is usually the beginning of phase 3. In this part you are still very much under the influence of the mushroom. This is a very sensitive part. You are vulnerable to influences during this time. Make sure you only experience positive things during this day. Stay away from social media. If you have a good meditation app or if you have recorded something ahead of time, this is a good time to use it. Recording things about your intentions, who you are, what you want to manifest, etc. is good to listen to right now. It will go very deep and work harder on your behalf. I do this. I have prerecorded messages for myself. Things about what I deserve, what I can allow, things about love, about safety, about my goals, my ideas are what I like to record. Make sure that people know not to bother you today. This is a good day for making sure you eat good clean food. It's a good time for a ritual bath, or teas. It's a good day for journaling and playing lo-fi music. It's a good day to smudge and physically clean out your space and open windows. Honoring your path and journey, your child, your healing, your body, these are the meditations today while the medicine still hums inside. Make reminders not to complain or say anything negative out loud during this sensitive period.

At the end of the day, microdose to help bring you down. Using the tea helps bring back some of the ibotenic acid and give you a lift while coming down from muscimol. High doses of amanita muscaria, like other entheogens, have their place. Once you begin working in this area my hope is that you learn what that place is. The changes can be profound. The healing can become hard to describe. The new ways you see the world, your intuition, your sense of self all become your ally in living without fear, solid in who you are with your dreams intact. The world can't wait to see it.t

CHAPTER 23   Smoking Amanita

The Elders and Time Travel

Once you have the mushroom voice onboard, have learned to hear the ancestors, and have some experience with time blips and managing time, I hope you experiment with smoking Amanita. It's really easy. You'll need a water pipe and a cracker dry Amanita, and just crush it up with your hand. After smoking for about an hour, listening to drums or sitting by a fire, or hopefully both, it's time for this meditation on time travel. It's an amazing tool.

A Meditation

I want you to read through this entirely while sober, and then save it for when you smoke Amanita. Understand that when you're smoking Amanita, everything I'm about to explain will happen rapidly. It's not like a guided meditation where they take you through imagery really slowly, and you watch it play out on the movie screen inside your mind. My point in sharing it in this book is for you to understand the imagery so that then when you do smoke it, you'll know what it is that you're supposed to do. Ideally, you'll smoke a lot of Amanita for a good hour before you close your eyes and lay down, and just put yourself through this process.

First, get situated where you don't have things bothering you or annoying you, and let people know that you need to be uninterrupted for at least the next ten minutes. Turn the ringer off on your phone, or better yet, get it out of the room completely. If you want to lay down, lay down. Just get comfortable, close your eyes and feel whatever you're sitting or lying on.

Picture the flame of a candle, and then bring two more candles into it so that the flames meet and you get a really big flame. Bring that flame closer and closer to your forehead to where your third eye would be, and feel the warmth of it. Count down from three to one, and then pop it right into your head. Imagine the flame inside your head glowing and filling you up, lighting your inner mind.

And now I want you to make that flame smaller and smaller and smaller and smaller until it goes out. And now there's just a wisp of smoke. Ahead of you, you see an elevator door. Walk towards it. When you arrive at the elevator door, you see that there's only one button, and it's a down button. Push it.

The door opens. The floor is glowing, and there's a hum. Step inside and turn around. Again, there's only one button, and that's a down button. Push it. The door closes, you hear the hum, and everything is blue. You can feel the elevator start to descend as you take in the blue hue of the light from the floor and the soft hum buzzing in your ears.

The elevator starts speeding up. You're going down faster and faster. Faster and faster and faster and faster and faster. All of a sudden, it slows to a stop. The doors open, and now everything outside of that elevator is glowing red.

Step off of the elevator and turn around to look behind you. The doors close. Everything around you is still red. Turn back around to look ahead of you. You see a moving walkway. Walk toward that and step onto it.

You feel it carrying you forward at a steady, comfortable pace. The elevator door shrinks into the distance, and you're surrounded by red light and that familiar hum as you continue being carried further still on the moving walkway. Look down to see that, in fact, the walkway is no longer holding you up. It's off in the distance behind you, and you're simply floating weightlessly through space. Look to your left and see that it is your past. Look to your right and see that it is your future.

First, look into your past on the left and see yourself as a child running and laughing with the wind in your hair. Move along that line to that day, to that child running and laughing. As you approach, reach out and stop that child. They look at you, and they're out of breath. You say, "Hi, I'm you in the future." See how they respond.

You're going to give that child three pieces of advice of your choosing. Make sure they know this is serious business. Get them to look you in the eye and really take in what you're saying. Get them to repeat it back to you to make sure they've got it. Give them an opportunity to ask clarifying questions to make sure they didn't misunderstand.

Then, let them go.

Suddenly you're being pulled away from them back along that timeline, back toward the future faster and faster and faster until you are back in the center again.

Now, look to your right at the future you. This is a future you that is living your dream life. If you could have literally any situation, anything in the world, this is what you want. They did it. You did it. You got there. And now you're going to go visit them. Move along that timeline to get to them until you reach them.

It's morning. What are you wearing? What does your bed look like? How does your bedroom look? What is your morning routine? When you open the blinds, you look out the window. What are you looking at? Who's with you? What does your kitchen look like? What are you making to drink? Is anyone else there? What do you do for money? How do you support yourself? What are you going to do today? What does that look like? How are you going to get there? Walking, biking, mass transit, car, what does it look like? How do you feel? Are you confident? Are you content? Who answers to you? Who do you answer to? How many people are around you? How many people do you have to deal with? What other living things are around you in your daily life? What are you wearing when you go out into the world? What does it feel like to be you? What worries and fears are gone? What are you so happy about? What drives you? What about at the end of the day? What do you do for dinner? Where do you eat it? Who prepared it? Who is with you? What's your bedtime routine?

Tap that person on the shoulder, make eye contact with them and say, "You actually did it. Can you please give me three pieces of advice on how you made this happen?" and then listen to what they have to say. Thank them, and then notice you're being pulled away back along your timeline. You're getting pulled away to the present. Hover here for a moment in stillness. Take your child and your future self. Pull them off the timeline and swing them out in front of you until they meet in front of you.

Watch them pass each other and keep going until they've traded places. Continue sending them around you until they meet behind you, pass each other, swing back to the timeline, and keep moving until they're in front of you. Watch them circle around you, passing each other in front of you, then behind you, then in front again, then behind again. See them spinning faster and faster and faster. Leave them there spinning and pull yourself upward. Look down below and watch them spinning as you see them disappear in the distance as you float away.

You are now completely off your timeline. You are your own sovereign moment, unencumbered by time or anything you've done in your timeline. You have taken a pause from your timeline. They're still spinning. Just hang here and take a break for a moment. Now, slowly descend back to where you were, situated right in the center of the circles they're tracing, and see their spin slow down until they finally land each on their own timeline. Turn around and see that the moving walkway is coming back to you again, and it's getting closer. You're on the walkway now, and you're moving. Everything is red and glowing and humming. In the distance, you can see the elevator. It's getting closer.

Step off the floating walkway and approach the elevator. Again, there's only one button. It's an up button. Push it. Doors open. Step inside, and turn around. One button, the up button. Push it. Everything is glowing blue. That blue hum. The elevator picks up speed as it gains altitude until you're going faster than you've ever gone before. Suddenly it slows to a stop. The doors open. Step out. Open your eyes.

This is the meditation to time travel. When you do that, after smoking Amanita, you will change your present you because you gave your child the advice, and they took it, and they made changes. Those changes affected your present state of being. You changed your messaging that informed your future, and now you have the ability to pull yourself towards it.

If you've never had any experiences with this mushroom or others like it, I know how all of this sounds. Believe me, I do. The sooner you start with Amanita, the sooner you're going to start seeing differences in your life. Being a scientist myself, I want to know how it works. I want to make sense of it. I need the details. But, no matter how I put it, nothing will make more sense than for me to just tell you that once you start doing it, it will make sense to you. The web-like nature of all of the stuff in this book will start to work together, and you'll begin to get an understanding of how it all works. There are some things you're just going to know, and you're going to get it, feel it, understand it, and then you're going to start sliding and moving through time and wielding it. And your life will never be the same because you'll never be the same.

PART 3
Tea Party!

ENDNOTE i

Love Letters

I've started working with the Amanita, over them I prayed.
"What do you have to teach me?" To them, I sang.
Dehydrate, decarboxylate, in the kitchen we danced;
our friendship enhanced.
"To be a hollow little bone," of them, I asked.
If you speak to me I will be still, quiet, and listen.
So I sit in meditation each and every day.
Drop into my heart space, this is what they say,
"Slow down Amanda, you're moving too fast.
You've been wounded Amanda, at this pace you won't last.
You must first heal yourself and care for your responsibilities.
Your first job is as a mother, so love her.
Prioritize your time, promote love within your home."
The Amanita brought me back to my roots,
my 1-2-3's, my daily routines, my A-B-C's.
I was up in the clouds scrambling frantically,
but in reality my dreams will unfold naturally,
when we are healthy mentally.
See, we've been through a lot collectively,
my presence in this home, a necessity.
Entrepreneurial dreams will be there for me,
 but won't mean anything, if my family is not healthy and happy.
Thanks to Amanita coaching my vision is more clear,
I'm grateful - everything I need is right here!
I'm grounded with less fear, anxiety starts to disappear,
and I'm more connected to my higher self.

— *Amanda Heals*

While visiting friends abroad on my 69th birthday, I tested positive for Covid. My legally mandated isolation and recovery allowed me the opportunity to immerse myself in my friends' beautiful homes and gardens. In a moment of awakening, I realized I was burned out and needed to step away from my busy-ness at home to take time to heal from multiple traumas and overwork throughout my life. After two powerful plant medicine sacred ceremonies, I found Amanita Dreamer, joined her Mushroom Voice Community, and soon began my Amanita journey. The healing is deep and reaches into my dreams and visions. Now I feel an overall sense of well-being and no longer need to please others because I am loving myself and don't need validation from the outside world.

— *Ana F.*

Everybody certainly remembers those 1970's grammar cartoons, like Conjunction Function. Amanita welcomes learning in the same way, for those who strive for the copacetic balance between handling business, while also enjoying life. Your points of view open tenfold, and your perspectives continue to expand with the all-encompassing universe.

Just like the array of train tracks in the cartoon, Amanita miraculously makes everything work out just right. Setting your intentions before the ceremony is essential. Bring up your intent throughout the experience. You're the engineer. Amanita will help guide you toward an ultimately positive destination. You have always had the keys to the universe, Amanita is there to remind you, that the keys have always been right there in your hands.

Amanita is an additive "like this and that". Amanita is like having a good friend who is always happy to see you. In fact, she may stop in like a gentle breeze, speaking directly to you, before going her way again. Offering a voice that is crystal clear, yet omnisciently patient. "We have been waiting for you." As she lets you know, her world is your world too. "Why don't you visit here more often", she says smiling, and her sense of humor will certainly make you smile too.

An infinitely short duration of time may pass before Amanita speaks again. The unspoken, a place where statements seem vain at last. The ole Irish gift of the gab, have you much? Even the Blarney Stones' most faithful patrons have their moments of silence, spaced in between the syllables. That is where the sound of the river gently rolling, the crickets and cicadas sing a rare and different tune, where all harmonies stay true.

When you have a choice like "this 'or' that." Reminding yourself of the intent throughout the ceremony, allows you to be the orchestrator of the grand symphony. Maybe you would like to increase your memory, just ask Amanita and she will provide the effervescent platitudes that are impossible to forget. Maybe you prefer to work on your sleep habits, then a pleasant evening at ease and rest awaits you, along with a labyrinth of yawns to induce the mood.

Milk and honey, bread and butter, peas and rice and making them run right. Right! The entirely opposite spectrum of just chillin' and chillaxing. Amanita also knows that sometimes you may want to be more productive. If you express this verbally to Amanita, you're going to be busier than a bumble bee and your honeycomb will ooze forth in a tastefully prolific fashion. If you prefer to be one with nature, all your senses will suddenly be heightened, and you may wake up to find out that you are the song that the morning brings.

Jerry Garcia once said there were huge capital letters that spelled "ALL" at his function, while Bob Marley's universally appealing statement, ONE LOVE", expanded that same perspective even further. Amanita runs diagnostics on you, and this reassurance brings your symbiotic existence with the entire universe to the forefront, accentuating the exquisite beauty that has been embedded, long ago, deep within your soul.

Without you even being totally aware of it, Amanita must lead you into a classroom. Where the great teachings may now commence. Out of the frying pan and into the fire. Let's go up the mountains or down to the seas. When meeting or parting with a dear friend like Amanita, "you should always say thank you or at least say please." Just like the sing-song rhymes that add their rhythmic conclusion to the tail end of the trains in the Conjunction Function, "I'm going to get you there if you are very careful". That is exactly what Amanita has planned for you.

— *K.C.*

I started dosing with A. Muscaria one month ago and since then, everything has changed. The first week with her was spent grieving. At first, I didn't understand what I was grieving, but then it became very clear. I was grieving all the times I gave away my personal power. I felt great sadness about this, so much, that I spent several days crying but also giving myself permission to have these feelings. Then, I made a promise to myself to never give my personal power away again. But the thing is – I found I didn't have to make a promise. It just came naturally now.

I speak up when something doesn't sit well with me. For the past 40 years of my life, I've tended to stay quiet as a way of not making drama even when things are bothering me. Now, if I don't like the way something is being handled or something is going, I have no problem speaking my mind. I say no to things that will be a waste of time for me. People used to say I was so "easygoing," but I now see that was just me being passive because I was afraid to speak up. I've even had people say, "What happened? You're so different now."

This has even affected my business. I have a small business that does "okay," but I've had a lack of drive for several years now and haven't made much progress. Now, things feel totally different. I have a feeling that I need to move forward with my business, get my name out there, and generally feel a sense of purpose that's been missing from my life for a long time. I've been spending more time working on my business than I have since I first opened it – plus I'm enjoying putting in the work.

— *Alex, California*

I came across Amanita Muscaria from watching a YouTube chat with Amanita Dreamer explaining the benefits and her own experience with the mushroom. I then went searching and came across the mushroom in a forest nearby in Ireland near me. I brought it home, followed a video on Amanita dreamer's website and I boiled a tea down following her steps. I sipped it slowly not knowing what to expect. Within minutes I felt relaxed, at ease, clarity and all feelings of anxiety gone. I had the best sleep of my life that night and woke up feeling so rested. I haven't had it since but do plan on trying it again. It also had a pleasantly sweet taste. I love this mushroom.

— *Anthony, Oregon*

Amanita Muscaria came to me through some mystical inner calling. I became obsessed with it, wanting to look at photos of it and learn about it. The Amanita Dreamer videos helped me recognize its potential to help those of us who have had traumatic childhoods. I am extremely sensitive, and I often work with flower essences. To me, Amanita feels like a patient, kind older man sitting with me on a simple wooden bench, helping me feel like I'm safe and have everything I need. As a massage therapist and herbalist, I typically use a variety of herbs in combinations customized for my clients. Two drops of Amanita flower essence in the massage oil typically helps them feel a safe and simple sort of contentment. Like it's saying, Need a nap? Here's a blanket. Want a cookie?

— *Brenda Fullick Wise, LMT, Green Thumbs Massage*

I have been working with Gerti in her first group of micro dosing Amanita Muscaria and have had a healing of a lifetime and it went from personal to collective. After finding my dose and receiving the effects of gentle calming of the raw state I was in, the self-regulating began with true ease and grace.

STORY: I had been visited by the past that week, visions, memories, emotions and feelings and I thought I was doing something wrong as I had spent years working through this trauma. The night of the spring solstice and full moon I was awake all night with constant input from the past and barely slept. Waking early to go do dog care, I curled up on the sofa to relax and gather my focus for the day. I entered a lucid state where I saw a woman with a non-descript dress decorated with what appeared to be wild strawberries on her bodice, who looked down and saw splotches of blood coming from under her dress being absorbed by the earth and when she looked up the red on the bodice were gone. This vision came back all week and revealed the healing of my life at the age of 66. The blood was my menstrual blood and was received by ancients present to celebrate me as a woman. I had been raped at 12 and the next morning my menstrual started and I never once celebrated the sacred rite of passage, but Amanita gave me what I needed. Later that week the discovery of the red on the bodice and the fact that they slid off when I looked down were the betrayals I was releasing.

Gerti told me that Amanita gives you what you need. And it is exactly in that moment what I needed more than anything else.

EXPERIENCE: The very first day I took only 4 drops and sat on my sofa and waited to see and notice what would occur. Within the first few minutes I felt a weight come over me, like a literal lead jacket on my shoulders and as I sat and the weight took over and gently pushed me further into my body I heard one word, "grounded". I realized it was the first time in so long I had felt this that I could not say with any accuracy when was the last time I had felt grounded. Amanita became the constant loving companion of everything that transpired afterwards with her hand on my back, telling me I had this and her loving embrace all-ways holding me.

— *C. Picolo*

My story is of an addiction to opiates such as fentanyl. Innocently addicted, my drug dealer was my doctors. Twenty years and five kids later I was finally able to stop the prescribed drugs when I started learning about Amanita and decided to give it a go. I weaned myself completely off all opiates in 2019 and haven't touched them since. I could not have done it without my sweet Amanita.

— *H. Frey*

This magical being has been a source of curiosity for me since I was young, introduced by the children's stories I read and movies I watched but innocently thought was part of the fable rather than true. In my 20's I found out that this master mushroom really existed and in my 30's she came into my reality through a dear friend and facilitator of this mushroom in ceremony. Although the time never aligned for me to have a ceremony with her, I felt closer to the mushroom. One day three or four years ago, a new friend from Sweden, showed up with a box of dried amanita that he had picked and dried for me a gift. I was beyond excited and started playing, eating small bites and larger bites during the day or before sleep and although sometimes felt a little more activated I always enjoyed the deep peace and calm that ensued. My dreams became clearer and easier to remember.

Then one year later another, another friend from Lithuania gifted me a tub of encapsulated amanita as a gift for the healing I had given him and suggested I try these tiny doses before bed. I was guided to take it once a week on a Friday evening and found myself sleeping deeper and longer than I had been able to do. Over the next 3 months I continued my weekly regime and could feel myself dropping deeper into my body with more rest, presence, and peace. I noticed that I felt bubbled by a peaceful presence, and I was able to tolerate large noisy crowds on Saturdays without feeling overwhelmed or overstimulated which was a dream come true after being so sensitive and hyperaware my whole life. Although this sensitivity was a gift for my healing work it also drained me.

After a big plant and mushroom conference where the amanita was given a tiny bit of airspace, and being introduced to Amanita dreamer by another friend, I became focused on what this mushroom was here to do for humanity. I could hear her encouraging me to dig deeper, to take a chance, that this beauty could be the answer I was looking for to help me and my clients to heal on a profound level. One of my values is to make medicine and healing accessible to all but being an acupuncturist there are only so many hours in the day I can work.

As I began my self-study with the videos and literature on Amanita dreamer and other sites, I understood why this mushroom was calling me. I have known that our nervous system needs regulating for a long time and have received and given acupuncture treatments for over 20 years to assist with that. But with the pace of life increasing as it is, going for and receiving treatments is not sustainable or self-empowering. I continued with my own bioassays for the next 3 months and experienced two main areas that sparked more interest.

In eastern philosophy we know that our internal and external environment are in constant communication and for harmony in health they must remain in flow. Just like the external, the internal environment is made up of elements such as fire and water. I've noticed the amanita brings the elements of water and fire back in balance in the body, reducing the fire symptoms such as anxiety, insomnia, PTSD, nervousness and increasing ease and grace. I have a long history of chronic sympathetic nervous arousal since birth, and I was guided to keep taking the amanita weekly.

My healing dropped deeper into my body, and I had over 4 months of long sleeps, more daytime rest, less socialising, and more silence. It was challenging at first as my fast-paced life did not match my new state but to be honest, I just did not have the energy. After 4 months I questioned whether there was anything else that I needed to investigate (as I was a little worried, I was never going to feel energised again) and had some tests done by my functional medicine doctor but all was clear. I was just learning how to be, instead of do!

The second strong experience I had was with inflammation in my fingers. 9 months after starting my protocol, and coming into winter, I noticed that my middle finger and my little finger (on the heart and pericardium channels) were inflamed and tender. I wondered if it was due to dampness in the environment (I live in the Balearic Islands in the Mediterranean) but the location of the inflammation was particularly interesting. As I continued my protocol it reduced and my left middle finger and little became swollen. I knew then this was not dampness but some deeper healing on my heart. The fingers are the ends of the channels and symptoms here usually indicate there is something deeper on its way out. I understood that this was the trauma of excess fire of anxiety and survival in my heart which was now healing, and I trusted the process.

So, my journey with my clients began with small doses without expectation and the results were unanimous. They all started to feel more able to integrate what they were sharing and experiencing with me, needing less treatments, slept deeper and/or longer and felt more at peace with themselves and their family units which was particularly appreciated by the parents among us. Some of my clients were more sensitive than others and like me, a small micro dose of dried amanita once a week influenced them for many days, whilst others needed to take it twice a week. Some, like me, found that taking the mushroom two nights in a row amplified their dream state so instead of feeling as grounded the next day they felt lighter and floatier which in itself was not an undesired effect but not what they needed at the time.

This was all encouraging, so I dived deeper into the medicine by making the tinctures as instructed. And these have had more consistent results, with the ability to help clients feel calm and sleep. I have tested even smaller doses with my 11-year-old son who has gone from being a light sleeper since he was a baby to now having deep restful sleeps every night. He now looks forward to his weekly dose and is also feeling a deep love for the dried amanita in my glass jars! I have witnessed two chronic insomniacs in their 40's with trauma around sleep, learn how to trust bedtime and sleep. A lot! This fills me with hope and inspiration, and I have started sharing this divine master medicine with more adults as I believe everyone has an overstimulated nervous system, with plans to speak to more parents about their children's sleeping habits.

I have always been able to represent those that need their voice to be heard. From humans, it has become the plants and trees and it was the glorious amanita that helped me hear that voice of the mushrooms 2 years ago. Since then, I have been working with functional mushroom and psilocybin with myself and clients in medicinal ways to remember love and joy as an innate state of being.

— *Dipika*

The A. muscaria mushroom found me at a time where I felt stuck and like life had slowed to a crawl. I was hesitant at first (not having much experience with entheogens), but eventually the call got so strong I felt compelled to start experimenting. I was blown away. It started with a few nice days of increased willpower and appreciation for life, and later moved on to some spiritual experiences on higher doses which have liberated me from a lot of worries (particularly related to time). It's my experience that this mushroom is simultaneously both incredibly practical and spiritual and cannot recommend it enough for anybody who feels like they would benefit from more energy, reduced anxiety, and/or its other benefits.

— *Jackson*

First off, I want to say that I am not a recreational user of anything sacred. I try and adhere to this. And sacred is how I view any healing medicine or entheogen. Therefore, I try to prepare myself spiritually before I partake. I've only used Amanita a handful of times with low doses each time. I eat them from the bag dry. This has worked good for me but there may be a better way. My feelings of Amanita are positive so far. In time I would like to do a heroic dose, but I don't feel ready. Amanita seems to be and enhancer in the ways I like. It boosts my energy and creativity; it can help me to fall asleep often with interesting lucid dreams. The glow I feel from it is nice and pleasant. Again, I've only taken small doses, about half of a two-to-four-inch button dry. Lastly, I love the taste.

— *Jalaboman*

My name is Lorraine. In March 2023, I started using Amanita Muscaria mushrooms in the form of a tea (15 g dried Amanita Muscaria with 250 ml water, heated for 20 minutes). I am microdosing 10 ml daily. Immediately, I have seen improvements in sleep, dreaming, lifted mood from depression, and increased energy.

— *Lorraine*

Thank you for being a voice to help assist so many of us, to beautiful support in healing our amazing bodies naturally and healthily. The awesome mushroom is assisting me in sleeping better and helping me fall in love with myself. I am having a relationship with nature in our oneness that is always meant to be. We just didn't know how to do it. This is one way to make this possible. it is also making a difference in calming my brain as I have come off treacherous medications. Now I have hope and know the reality of restored health in its original state is possible! And I am experiencing it! I am so happy!

— *L.H., the Midwest*

I was amazed when I discovered amanita muscaria. I watched your videos about how to take it. I bit the bullet after I saw you smoke it and eat it raw. I also saw a Russian man eat one raw. So, I did it. I thought I might die, but nope I'm still here. Eating raw amanita muscaria is what I prefer. I feel I don't lose anything from the mushroom. I may do a lil' lemon tek in my mouth when I drink lemon water and eat a mushroom. But that's about it. I love them raw.

I went through more this year than any other time in my life. Amanita makes me fearless. A new landlord cut down a lemon tree that I had had for over ten years. I had been taking amanita muscaria for almost a year at this point I microdose raw almost every day. I had never harnessed so much anger and frustration and just let I go in a rage; I've never yelled so loudly, and this went on for months as they continued to not treat me well. I almost got evicted. but instead of taking a backseat to my emotions like normally; I would just hold it in... this time I let it out and it was intense but controlled.

When I thought that I was going to be evicted and separated from my dog I cried so deeply, I have never cried like that in my life. I felt that I could go down the spiral of crying so low that it was almost bottomless, and I could keep going down the hole with the tears streaming down my face. but I knew I had to grieve a certain amount; otherwise, I could make myself sick... but it was beautiful in how I cleaned up/felt those emotions, it's like going in a big house, with all these doors to rooms that you have never been in but are a part of you. rooms that are dark, that contain scenes from your life. Amanita Muscaria allows you to open those doors and shed light on the scenes that went on in your life, things that you wanted to forget. Its spirit holds your hand and go's in with you. It allows you to remember... and move on.

Amanita muscaria also puts me at ease with the current events in the world. In the middle of a crisis amanita makes you feel chill and calm. it's an island on a raging sea. I also like cannabis. amanita muscaria is cannabis on steroids for me. and when I do them together its bliss. I also do ORMUS, which is also amazing.

I play guitar and piano and sing, and amanita muscaria gives me confidence to sing loud and just gets rid of performing fear. To "soma" it up, I'll say that amanita muscaria is fearless and that's how I will live the rest of my days FEARLESS!!!!!!!!!!!!!!

Thank YOU, DREAMER, you're the best!!!!!

— *Michael C.*

Amanita completely changed my life. I had been wanting to stop drinking and smoking for years but never could muster the will power for very long (been drinking since I was 12 and I'm now 42.) Amanita came to my attention via some very special spiritual friends 2 years ago. I didn't try it, but it came onto my radar then and made an impression. A year later one of the friends arrived at my place with some freshly dried Amanitas he had harvested. My father had just passed, and I was looking for some big shifts and wanted to be more serious about my artistic career. Interestingly shortly after the mushrooms came into the living room, I became sleepy and fell into a deep sleep for 16 hours (I believe because I had been heavily drinking the day before and I somehow "knew" I needed to detox before I partook. Upon waking (on Christmas eve ironically) I took my first very small dose just a bite (about the size of half my thumb.) I knew how important it is not to drink when ingesting Amanita, so I didn't consume any alcohol. What was damn near miraculous was that I completely stopped carving alcohol and Marijuana almost immediately within 24 hours and my 72 all craving was just gone. I was shocked as I really didn't expect it to work, but my intention was truly very sincere. I was completely blown away. I have stayed totally sober since and continue to dose a couple days a month and it is working. I tell my friends these days that when they are truly ready to quit, I can help them… or rather my helper can. I'm so grateful to Amanita, it's a travesty that it's been suppressed and noted as poisonous as it really is the antidote to it. I think Amanita is an incredible medicine and I believe it is the greatest cure for addiction on the planet currently.

— *R.L., Texas*

I came across AD and the mushroom by chance, a podcast sparked my interest. It was the tail end of a 3-year unravelling of my life and ego. I felt that I had lost my way and had suffered from a series of breakdowns. I had concluded that there was no way to have a sense of purpose, and that every life, past present and future is an identical copy of the last with any sense of choice being an illusion. I did some research and began to "find my dose" I found I was sleeping loads and felt some mild effects on larger doses but no emotional shift. Then out of the blue a couple of days after I had slept for 48 hours straight, I had a profound realisation. Fear had dominated my entire life down to the smallest detail. Up until that point I was pretty sure I had overcome many adversities. But I had never experienced the emotional significance of gratification, in line with the conquering of fear. Now when I micro dose I feel emboldened. It is early days for me, but I can already see things starting to shift. I should add that I had also been practicing compassionate enquiry using breath work and meditation and will continue to do these things in line with using amanita.

— *Spacehaul*

I've seen Kärpässieni (literally "the fly mushroom" in Finnish) around every year since my childhood here in Finland. Everybody learns that it's not to be touched, that it's extremely bad for you, if not outright "deadly". Still, all those historical accounts of its shamanic use here suggested curiously otherwise. Then, after decades of yearly encounters with the mushroom, I found Amanita Dreamer's wonderful website and the Fly Agaric book that Kevin Feeney had edited. These two things were very inspirational and eye-opening. I studied the basics thoroughly and started microdosing. The effects are clear: Amanita muscaria has been very beneficial to the quality of my sleep. It has also clearly been good for the general mood and energy. In addition to microdosing with Amanita tea, I've successfully used Amanita ointment for psoriasis. It's great that this information is out there! Thank you for your work!

— *Tapio*

I found Amanita Dreamer by accident several months ago. Intrigued by her story I wondered if this medicine might help me with my depression and ADHD. I had been taking meds for a year and had very recently decided to stop, as they made me feel terrible even though they seemed to help my symptoms of ADHD. I ordered Amanita and followed Dreamer's instructions precisely for micro dosing. I was so shocked by the results that I unexpectedly had! I have spent my entire long adult life verbally abusing myself through continuous negative browbeating self-talk. I don't think I went 15 minutes without saying something denigrating to myself. It was horrible and unchanging… until Amanita. The afternoon after my second dose, I was feeding my animals and it dawned on me, "Every time I try to say something vile to myself, a voice immediately interjects and corrects me!" I wrote it off thinking it was some kind of fluke, I was so afraid to even hope that this was possible. This kept happening every day until, I kid you not, the verbal abuse stopped! I finally let myself believe the change might be permanent and to this day I am still free from that demon! This may seem trivial, but it plagued me. It was awful and I am smart enough to understand how deeply ingrained that was into my subconscious and years of personal work and therapy had not abolished it. I am so grateful and blessed. I continue to micro and macro, though not regularly. It is kind of strange how it seems that sacred medicine gets right in and goes to work, helping us to shed the unnecessary and the untrue without becoming a crutch. True freedom! If that is the only thing I gain, it is monumental. Thank you, Dreamer, for your brave and unwavering dedication to serve your fellow travelers. Much love.

— *Taasha, Oregon*

ENDNOTE ii — *References*

Ch 3 - What Is This Mushroom?

Voynova, Maria, et al. "Toxicological and Pharmacological Profile of Amanita Muscaria (L.) Lam. – a New Rising Opportunity for Biomedicine." Pharmacia, Bulgarian Pharmaceutical Scientific Society, 26 Nov. 2020, https://pharmacia.pensoft.net/article/56112/.

Ch 4 - Using the Mushroom

Kim, Jin, et al. "The Toxicological Pathologic Study of Amanita Muscaria in Sprague-Dawley Rat." Journal of Life Science, vol. 19, no. 8, 2009, pp. 1152–1158., https://doi.org/10.5352/jls.2009.19.8.1152.

Masha, Baba. Microdosing with Amanita Muscaria: Creativity, Healing, and Recovery with the Sacred Mushroom. Park Street Press, 2022.

Zinkand, William C., et al. "Ibotenic Acid Mediates Neurotoxicity and Phosphoinositide Hydrolysis by Independent Receptor Mechanisms." Molecular and Chemical Neuropathology, vol. 16, no. 1-2, Feb. 1992, pp. 1–10., https://doi.org/10.1007/bf03159956.

Michelot, Didier, and Leda Maria Melendez-Howell. "Amanita Muscaria: Chemistry, Biology, Toxicology, and Ethnomycology." Mycological Research, vol. 107, no. 2, Feb. 2003, pp. 131–146., https://doi.org/10.1017/s0953756203007305.

Ch 10 - Sleep

Penzel, Thomas, et al. "Dynamics of Heart Rate and Sleep Stages in Normals and Patients with Sleep Apnea." Neuropsychopharmacology, vol. 28, no. S1, 1 July 2003, https://doi.org/10.1038/sj.npp.1300146.

Fan, Xiaojun, et al. "The Effects of Ventilation and Temperature on Sleep Quality and next-Day Work Performance: Pilot Measurements in a Climate Chamber." Building and Environment, vol. 209, 14 Dec. 2021, p. 108666., https://doi.org/10.1016/j.buildenv.2021.108666.

Ch 13 - Sun, Water, Fire, and Earth

Sasaki, Hiroshi, et al. "UV-B Exposure to the Eye Depending on Solar Altitude." Eye & Contact Lens: Science & Clinical Practice, vol. 37, no. 4, July 2011, pp. 191–195., https://doi.org/10.1097/icl.0b013e31821fbf29.

Ch 22 - High Dosing

Trent, Austin. "Method for Producing Muscimol and/or Reducing Ibotenic Acid from Amanita Tissue - Patent US-8784835-B2 - Pubchem." National Center for Biotechnology Information. PubChem Compound Database, U.S. National Library of Medicine, 22 July 2014, https://pubchem.ncbi.nlm.nih.gov/patent/US-8784835-B2.

Feeney, Kevin M. "Chapter 4." Fly Agaric: A Compendium of History, Pharmacology, Mythology & Exploration, Fly Agaric Press, Ellenburg, WA, 2020, pp. 58–62.

ENDNOTE iii

Appendix A

If you're having trouble finding your dose, or if you're experiencing something not optimal and the graphics in the book don't help, read this.

You are free to experiment. The dosing and protocol language in this book is meant to help allay fears and guide folks to learn what harm reduction practices look like. Work on taking more or less. Work on converting it further into more muscimol or using it with less conversion. If you have been taking it every day for a week, maybe it's time to let your body rest with some days in between. If you have only been taking it every few days, maybe you need more. The optimal dose is the one where you feel better without overdoing it.

Ibotenic acid and its effects might be better understood through the lens of the fight or flight response instead of trying to memorize ibotenic acid's symptoms. That response takes blood flow away from our thinking cortex in the brain and brings it inward to the mid-bran where we react or use our thoughts less and do what comes more naturally. It diverts energy and blood flow from the gut toward the extremities so we can run or act and have what we need to do that. Vison gets sharper and we become more physical, primed to expend more energy and work. Knowing this, ibotenic acid's response to help you go into hyper focus and able to function also come with excitability of the muscles, nerves and blood flow to our arms and legs, and could cause the digestive issues.

The opposite of this would be the rest and digest, safety, living through the heart and calmness of the other side of this cycle where we are not in danger but are safe. This is where we return to digestion and relax the need for hyperfocus or all that availability to our arms and legs. We can now return to normal life, sleeping, doing mundane tasks and focusing on math or reading or paying the bills. Too much of this thing can bring us down into states of extreme fatigue and being lethargic, like heaviness and like we are slogging through mud. *If* you view muscimol through that lens, it may help you to find ways to play with your dosing to learn what you need.

The ADHD brain of course reacts differently to this and with ibotenic acid used by many in that community for the attention and focus, it can make it a little difficult to find your way and indeed many in our community have learned of their neurotype because of ibotenic acid's effect and they sought a diagnosis, and it was part of their healing journey. When you add the ADHD neurotype that has paradoxical effects to stimulants it can be even more difficult.

I've also created a private community of folks who use this mushroom. We meet weekly and on weekends. Some of the themes are ADHD, Entheogenic High Dosing, Show and Tell, Dance Party, Open Topic/Q&A about Dosing, Shamanism Guidance, Practitioner's Meeting, and Integration Counseling, among others. It is a loving and safe space for everyone, and many people learn how to find their best doses, how to find some more help, or find someone to help them through a high dose journey. You can find this community at MushroomVoice.com

Lastly, you can look up "what does _____ do in the body" and put glutamate, choline, and GABA in that blank one at a time, and read about those effects. When you put ibotenic acid in place of glutamate or choline and muscimol where GABA is in your mind, it may better help you understand your body effects to the dosing. Remember, as of the publication of this book, there are no studies so there is nothing to really search for what this mushroom does to the human body. Most of what is online right now are poorly interpreted studies or very old and based on outdated research about glutamate, choline or GABA. Or it is about synthetic isolated ibotenic acid or muscimol. The science of glutamate, choline and GABA is changing rapidly which is good, but ibotenic acid and muscimol is not so much.

ENDNOTE iv

Appendix B

DAY	Dose Taken	Time

Based on *how you feel right now*, no matter what time it is or when you took your dose, mark how intensely / frequently you experience these.

	−								+
Anxiety	⊖	·	·	·	·	·	·	·	⊕
Intrusive thoughts	⊖	·	·	·	·	·	·	·	⊕
Jumpiness	⊖	·	·	·	·	·	·	·	⊕
Muscle spasms	⊖	·	·	·	·	·	·	·	⊕
Restless legs	⊖	·	·	·	·	·	·	·	⊕
Lack of motivation	⊖	·	·	·	·	·	·	·	⊕
Cravings	⊖	·	·	·	·	·	·	·	⊕
Overwhelm	⊖	·	·	·	·	·	·	·	⊕
Trouble sleeping	⊖	·	·	·	·	·	·	·	⊕
Lack of Dreaming	⊖	·	·	·	·	·	·	·	⊕
Body aches	⊖	·	·	·	·	·	·	·	⊕
Hopelessness	⊖	·	·	·	·	·	·	·	⊕

Notes (changes, worries, fears, positives, what's happening in life, questions):

| DAY | Dose Taken | Time |

Based on *how you feel right now*, no matter what time it is or when you took your dose, mark how intensely / frequently you experience these.

Symptom	–									+
Anxiety	⊖	·	·	·	·	·	·	·	·	⊕
Intrusive thoughts	⊖	·	·	·	·	·	·	·	·	⊕
Jumpiness	⊖	·	·	·	·	·	·	·	·	⊕
Muscle spasms	⊖	·	·	·	·	·	·	·	·	⊕
Restless legs	⊖	·	·	·	·	·	·	·	·	⊕
Lack of motivation	⊖	·	·	·	·	·	·	·	·	⊕
Cravings	⊖	·	·	·	·	·	·	·	·	⊕
Overwhelm	⊖	·	·	·	·	·	·	·	·	⊕
Trouble sleeping	⊖	·	·	·	·	·	·	·	·	⊕
Lack of Dreaming	⊖	·	·	·	·	·	·	·	·	⊕
Body aches	⊖	·	·	·	·	·	·	·	·	⊕
Hopelessness	⊖	·	·	·	·	·	·	·	·	⊕

Notes (changes, worries, fears, positives, what's happening in life, questions):

DAY	Dose Taken	Time

Based on *how you feel right now*, no matter what time it is or when you took your dose, mark how intensely / frequently you experience these.

	−									+
Anxiety	⊖	·	·	·	·	·	·	·	·	⊕
Intrusive thoughts	⊖	·	·	·	·	·	·	·	·	⊕
Jumpiness	⊖	·	·	·	·	·	·	·	·	⊕
Muscle spasms	⊖	·	·	·	·	·	·	·	·	⊕
Restless legs	⊖	·	·	·	·	·	·	·	·	⊕
Lack of motivation	⊖	·	·	·	·	·	·	·	·	⊕
Cravings	⊖	·	·	·	·	·	·	·	·	⊕
Overwhelm	⊖	·	·	·	·	·	·	·	·	⊕
Trouble sleeping	⊖	·	·	·	·	·	·	·	·	⊕
Lack of Dreaming	⊖	·	·	·	·	·	·	·	·	⊕
Body aches	⊖	·	·	·	·	·	·	·	·	⊕
Hopelessness	⊖	·	·	·	·	·	·	·	·	⊕

Notes (changes, worries, fears, positives, what's happening in life, questions):

DAY	Dose Taken	Time

Based on *how you feel right now*, no matter what time it is or when you took your dose, mark how intensely / frequently you experience these.

	–									+
Anxiety	⊖	·	·	·	·	·	·	·	·	⊕
Intrusive thoughts	⊖	·	·	·	·	·	·	·	·	⊕
Jumpiness	⊖	·	·	·	·	·	·	·	·	⊕
Muscle spasms	⊖	·	·	·	·	·	·	·	·	⊕
Restless legs	⊖	·	·	·	·	·	·	·	·	⊕
Lack of motivation	⊖	·	·	·	·	·	·	·	·	⊕
Cravings	⊖	·	·	·	·	·	·	·	·	⊕
Overwhelm	⊖	·	·	·	·	·	·	·	·	⊕
Trouble sleeping	⊖	·	·	·	·	·	·	·	·	⊕
Lack of Dreaming	⊖	·	·	·	·	·	·	·	·	⊕
Body aches	⊖	·	·	·	·	·	·	·	·	⊕
Hopelessness	⊖	·	·	·	·	·	·	·	·	⊕

Notes (changes, worries, fears, positives, what's happening in life, questions):

DAY	Dose Taken	Time

Based on *how you feel right now*, no matter what time it is or when you took your dose, mark how intensely / frequently you experience these.

	⊖									⊕
Anxiety	⊖	·	·	·	·	·	·	·	·	⊕
Intrusive thoughts	⊖	·	·	·	·	·	·	·	·	⊕
Jumpiness	⊖	·	·	·	·	·	·	·	·	⊕
Muscle spasms	⊖	·	·	·	·	·	·	·	·	⊕
Restless legs	⊖	·	·	·	·	·	·	·	·	⊕
Lack of motivation	⊖	·	·	·	·	·	·	·	·	⊕
Cravings	⊖	·	·	·	·	·	·	·	·	⊕
Overwhelm	⊖	·	·	·	·	·	·	·	·	⊕
Trouble sleeping	⊖	·	·	·	·	·	·	·	·	⊕
Lack of Dreaming	⊖	·	·	·	·	·	·	·	·	⊕
Body aches	⊖	·	·	·	·	·	·	·	·	⊕
Hopelessness	⊖	·	·	·	·	·	·	·	·	⊕

Notes (changes, worries, fears, positives, what's happening in life, questions):

DAY	Dose Taken	Time

Based on *how you feel right now*, no matter what time it is or when you took your dose, mark how intensely / frequently you experience these.

	−									+
Anxiety	⊖	·	·	·	·	·	·	·	·	⊕
Intrusive thoughts	⊖	·	·	·	·	·	·	·	·	⊕
Jumpiness	⊖	·	·	·	·	·	·	·	·	⊕
Muscle spasms	⊖	·	·	·	·	·	·	·	·	⊕
Restless legs	⊖	·	·	·	·	·	·	·	·	⊕
Lack of motivation	⊖	·	·	·	·	·	·	·	·	⊕
Cravings	⊖	·	·	·	·	·	·	·	·	⊕
Overwhelm	⊖	·	·	·	·	·	·	·	·	⊕
Trouble sleeping	⊖	·	·	·	·	·	·	·	·	⊕
Lack of Dreaming	⊖	·	·	·	·	·	·	·	·	⊕
Body aches	⊖	·	·	·	·	·	·	·	·	⊕
Hopelessness	⊖	·	·	·	·	·	·	·	·	⊕

Notes (changes, worries, fears, positives, what's happening in life, questions):

DAY	Dose Taken	Time

Based on *how you feel right now*, no matter what time it is or when you took your dose, mark how intensely / frequently you experience these.

- Anxiety ⊖ · · · · · · · · ⊕
- Intrusive thoughts ⊖ · · · · · · · · ⊕
- Jumpiness ⊖ · · · · · · · · ⊕
- Muscle spasms ⊖ · · · · · · · · ⊕
- Restless legs ⊖ · · · · · · · · ⊕
- Lack of motivation ⊖ · · · · · · · · ⊕
- Cravings ⊖ · · · · · · · · ⊕
- Overwhelm ⊖ · · · · · · · · ⊕
- Trouble sleeping ⊖ · · · · · · · · ⊕
- Lack of Dreaming ⊖ · · · · · · · · ⊕
- Body aches ⊖ · · · · · · · · ⊕
- Hopelessness ⊖ · · · · · · · · ⊕

Notes (changes, worries, fears, positives, what's happening in life, questions):

| DAY | Dose Taken | | Time | |

Based on *how you feel right now*, no matter what time it is or when you took your dose, mark how intensely / frequently you experience these.

	⊖										⊕
Anxiety	⊖	·	·	·	·	·	·	·	·	·	⊕
Intrusive thoughts	⊖	·	·	·	·	·	·	·	·	·	⊕
Jumpiness	⊖	·	·	·	·	·	·	·	·	·	⊕
Muscle spasms	⊖	·	·	·	·	·	·	·	·	·	⊕
Restless legs	⊖	·	·	·	·	·	·	·	·	·	⊕
Lack of motivation	⊖	·	·	·	·	·	·	·	·	·	⊕
Cravings	⊖	·	·	·	·	·	·	·	·	·	⊕
Overwhelm	⊖	·	·	·	·	·	·	·	·	·	⊕
Trouble sleeping	⊖	·	·	·	·	·	·	·	·	·	⊕
Lack of Dreaming	⊖	·	·	·	·	·	·	·	·	·	⊕
Body aches	⊖	·	·	·	·	·	·	·	·	·	⊕
Hopelessness	⊖	·	·	·	·	·	·	·	·	·	⊕

Notes (changes, worries, fears, positives, what's happening in life, questions):

DAY	Dose Taken	Time

Based on *how you feel right now*, no matter what time it is or when you took your dose, mark how intensely / frequently you experience these.

- Anxiety ⊖ — — — — — — — — ⊕
- Intrusive thoughts ⊖ — — — — — — — — ⊕
- Jumpiness ⊖ — — — — — — — — ⊕
- Muscle spasms ⊖ — — — — — — — — ⊕
- Restless legs ⊖ — — — — — — — — ⊕
- Lack of motivation ⊖ — — — — — — — — ⊕
- Cravings ⊖ — — — — — — — — ⊕
- Overwhelm ⊖ — — — — — — — — ⊕
- Trouble sleeping ⊖ — — — — — — — — ⊕
- Lack of Dreaming ⊖ — — — — — — — — ⊕
- Body aches ⊖ — — — — — — — — ⊕
- Hopelessness ⊖ — — — — — — — — ⊕

Notes (changes, worries, fears, positives, what's happening in life, questions):

Macrodose #

Dose _____   How long before you felt something _____

Note what you felt as the time progressed

Which of the following did you experience?

Time Jumps   Bouts of Sadness
High Motivation   Confusion
Crying   Feeling Invincible
Multiple Timelines Laughter
Feeling High / Drunk Deep Thoughts
Dancing & Moving   Limp Arms / Legs

List other things you experienced

Macrodose

Dose   How long before you felt something

Note what you felt as the time progressed

Which of the following did you experience?

                Time Jumps   Bouts of Sadness
            High Motivation   Confusion
                      Crying   Feeling Invincible
           Multiple Timelines   Laughter
          Feeling High / Drunk   Deep Thoughts
          Dancing & Moving   Limp Arms / Legs

List other things you experienced

Macrodose #

Dose ▢   How long before you felt something ▢

Note what you felt as the time progressed

▢

Which of the following did you experience?

        Time Jumps   Bouts of Sadness
    High Motivation   Confusion
            Crying   Feeling Invincible
  Multiple Timelines   Laughter
  Feeling High / Drunk   Deep Thoughts
  Dancing & Moving   Limp Arms / Legs

List other things you experienced

▢

Macrodose

Dose   How long before you felt something

Note what you felt as the time progressed

Which of the following did you experience?

    Time Jumps   Bouts of Sadness
High Motivation   Confusion
Crying   Feeling Invincible
Multiple Timelines   Laughter
Feeling High / Drunk   Deep Thoughts
Dancing & Moving   Limp Arms / Legs

List other things you experienced

ENDNOTE V

Meet the Team

Amanita Dreamer AUTHOR

Amanita Dreamer is an educator on the Amanita muscaria mushroom. When she began in 2019, there was very little information about this mushroom, and what was available was inaccurate and harmful. She was planning her exit from the planet when the use of this mushroom saved her life. She has chosen to devote the rest of her life to helping others learn about the amazing power of this mushroom. She works to help others learn safe and effective ways to incorporate this medicine into their lives. With five years of her own use and experimentation, she brings her rigorous investigation into the research and science along with the aggregated anecdotal information from thousands in her community. She has developed rules and nomenclature around the use in small and large amounts, spiritual impacts, mind-altering growth, and potential uses. She has also posed many hypotheses on the complex medicine within. Finally, she has coined terms and ideas surrounding its ideology, use, community, and potential. In 2020 she launched the first line of products using this mushroom, with sales that continue to climb. To date, she has developed the world's largest online repository of Amanita muscaria information. She shares her work openly on public platforms, and once harsh censorship began, she continued on her own private platform, AmanitaDreamer.net. Knowing her audience, her aim is to cast a wide net and create helpful information that connects with as many different types of users of the material as possible, from the curious to those with a dire need, from the recreational user to those who are becoming medicine people in their communities. She works with corporations in the development of products and advises other content creators on accurate reporting. She helps practitioners learn how to help their clients through use and integration. She speaks at conventions, festivals, and societies, sharing her love of this medicine with all who will listen. In failing to keep up with the demands of the public, she created a community of people who also use the mushroom to collaborate and share their knowledge at MushroomVoice.com. She is currently filming a documentary and writing her next book. For wholesale and booking information, she can be found at *AmanitaDreamer.com*

Ryan Bayron DESIGNER

His two oldest friends are Curiosity and Playfulness, and he takes them with him wherever he goes. Thanks to them, he's collected quite an assortment of passions, skills, and party tricks. After a couple of years of undergrad music theory, Ryan took a 13-year break to get married, go broke, give a TEDx Talk, become a dad, co-host a podcast, publish a book, go not-broke, and amass a social media following by talking about therapy on TikTok. When the pandemic hit, he returned to finish his BFA in Cinematic Arts at the ripe young age of 35. A modern-day Jack-of-most-trades, he's collected a patchwork of disparate achievements, showables, and hey-look-what-I-dids that are as confusing as they are impressive. The one thing they all have in common? They reflect his passion for exploring what it means to be human (and also his ADHD).

If you have projects that you think Ryan could lend his expertise to, you can view his portfolio at *RyanBayron.com* and his multimedia production company (HappyBox Productions) at *hpybx.com*.

Tammi Barnes & Jason Cook EDITORS

Tammi and Jason edited the book for grammar, punctuation, and flow. I (Dreamer) found them on UpWork.com, and they have been the most amazing editors. As you may see, there are inconsistencies in some of this. I kept it that way to reflect the different choices and personalities of each of them.

Who Did What?

I teach this as a course online and I recorded the course for this book. Ryan put it through a transcription service and went through and edited it down into a readable manuscript. I went through his edits and omitted, rewrote, and changed it or left it.

If I felt like something wasn't worded right, he suggested better. If I felt like what he wrote wasn't what I was trying to say, I fixed it.

I drew out the worksheets and pages I wanted, and he formatted them.

When it was finished, I described the look I was going for in the layout and design of the book, and Ryan created it in various Adobe products. After he did the layout and visual design, I would show him the changes I wanted. Then, he would make those changes and offer ideas and input.

For the cover, I described the idea and image I wanted. I mailed him the items for the photo and he staged, shot, and edited it. We collaborated on the typography and arrangement of the final photo and cover.

Together I think we created something that will serve you well.

www.ingramcontent.com/pod-product-compliance
Lightning Source LLC
Chambersburg PA
CBHW080613230426
43664CB00019B/2872